The Witch's Journey

Other books by Moira Hodgkinson

Living Witchcraft

The Witch's Journey

A Practical Guide to Making Magic
and
Rituals that Work for You.

by

Moira Hodgkinson

Thoth Publications
Loughborough, United Kingdom

A CIP catalogue record for this book is available from the British Library.

Cover design by Avanson Design

ISBN 978-870450-76-8

Printed and bound in USA

Published by Thoth Publications
64 Leopold Street, Loughborough, LE11 5DN

Web address: www.thoth.co.uk
email: enquiries@thoth.co.uk

CONTENTS

ACKNOWLEGMENT

With Thanks and Love

This book would not have been possible without all the people who have come to my talks and workshops for guidance and teaching over the years, some of whom are now good friends. Those of you who ask the most basic questions or the more challenging ones and those who sit quietly at the back of the room, silently taking it all in, to each and every one of you I offer my heart-felt thanks. You give me inspiration, new insights, laughter and many blessings, keeping the path fresh and alive for me. This book is for you, I hope you enjoy it, thank you for your support and friendship.

Thanks to my husband and best friend, Chris, my daughter Phoebe and my family, Nikki & Ant, May, Jessica K, Cayt, Ian, the Sherwood Oak Circle, my friends at the many moots and camps, the staff and owners of the venues I work in and finally, to my friend Gordon for crowning me the world's first Jazz Witch.

INTRODUCTION

The earth we live on has been worshipped and respected for thousands of years all over the world - people lived in harmony with the forces of nature and relied on it for their very existence. The earth was seen not just as a useful resource to be utilised and harvested for our gain, but as a living being with its own spirit and energy systems. The Pagan faith of our ancestors left its mark in the form of the ancient stone circles and chalk figures that dot our countryside. Stonehenge and Avebury stone circles are just two of the most well-known examples and although there is still some speculation of their origins, when combined with the countless green-men and Sheila-na-gig statues that are so often found in or near Christian places of worship, it is clear that Britain has firm ties with the earth as the divine feminine and masculine spirit and those ties are not going away any time soon.

Paganism is a celebration of life and death, of the turning of the seasons and a way of expressing our passion and care for the earth and all of the living things we share it with. Our Celtic ancestors practiced folk magic and healing as a matter of course and it was seen as quite acceptable to do so. In the middle-ages witches were the village healers, the midwives and wise women. As practitioners of natural healing and magic, they came to be persecuted for their continuing belief in and celebration of the old Pagan deities during the rise of Christianity across Europe and Britain and many hundreds were tried at court and hanged for practising witchcraft, (apart from Scotland, witches were not burned at the stake in the UK). Much of this persecution was due to the mistaken belief that witches worshipped the Devil, despite the Devil being a Christian concept and bearing only a passing resemblance to the natural deities that were being revered before the Church started to enforce the practice of Christianity.

Paganism as a religion is going through a wave of increasing popularity right now, but what do we mean when we say it is an earth-based religion? How can we make a connection with the earth in a meaningful, spiritual way when every day we're confronted with the problems and stresses of our technological and commercial society, which is far removed from concept of living in harmony with the earth? It can be hard to live in a way that feels balanced and in tune with nature and contemporary Pagans feel that their faith allows this balance and sense of connection to the earth to be restored. To be at peace with our place in nature, to feel in harmony with the swell and tides of the seasons, to give thanks gracefully for what we take from the earth and to tap into its mysteries and energies to further bring harmony and peace - that is Paganism. Paganism brings us into contact with nature and allows us to develop a deeper connection and understanding with it and witchcraft is an extension of that, through which we can shape and form universal energies and use them to transform negative to positive and to heal ourselves, mind, body and soul.

Witchcraft, sometimes called Wicca, brings its followers a sense of oneness with the earth, with the essence of the divine, revering nature in all its forms and gives us as individuals an awareness of how to empower our lives. As witches, we are generally environmentally friendly and strive to be conscious of how our actions affect both other people, animals and the planet as a whole. Witchcraft encourages us to become more spiritually aware of and sensitive to universal and personal energies. Through our rituals, meditations and seasonal celebrations, we can learn how to use and work with these energies for positive change.

One of the principals of witchcraft is that of a belief in a goddess and god. The old gods of Paganism are the earth Goddess, a representation of female energies in three aspects of maiden, mother and crone, and the horned god as a representation of male energies. The Goddess is seen as the mother of all things, the life giver and the one who gives up her energy to produce the harvest. She gives life and also takes it away; she is a goddess of the seasons and the passing of time. The horned god also represents nature; He is both the horned stag of the forest and the hunter who tracks the stag down. Often pictured playing pipes or dancing a jig with a gleeful smile, the horned god is the embodiment of wild and joyful nature.

Very often, those who have come naturally to the craft will be eclectic in their outlook and may be Pagan, Witch, Wiccan, Heathen and Druid and use and adapt the practices they have learned from each to make their practice and rituals unique. The term wicca has been adopted by a vast proportion of newcomers to the craft who will generally have a particular path or book they use as a point of reference, a slightly formal way of sticking to it, often with a great fondness for big gatherings and witchy paraphernalia like velvet robes, crystal embedded wands and large, shiny pentagram pendants. There isn't anything wrong with this approach providing there is sincerity behind it and a certain level of knowledge, experience, understanding and study, rather than blindly following the rules and traditions that have been laid out already.

The term wicca can be useful in public environments as a more acceptable word for witch and many witches will call themselves wiccan to people in the real world simply because saying one is a witch often brings up negative associations one would rather avoid. Declaring your religion and instantly being asked if you are a white or black witch is annoying, if nothing else, and saying wicca instead of witch sometimes gets around this nicely. The general public en masse don't really know what being wiccan means and immediately ask for an explanation, offering us a brilliant opportunity to talk about honouring the earth, a fertility goddess and a god of the forests before getting round to the topic of spell casting and magic.

In general, I've found that those who use the word witch tend to have a more organic, instinctive quality to their magic and rituals than those who identify with wicca and aren't afraid to make it up as they go along, using whatever ingredients are ready to hand rather than exactly what the spell or recipe calls for. Actually, we are less inclined to use a given spell or ritual in the first place, preferring to come up with our own, intuitive ways of working, either in a small coven or as solitaries, sometimes coming together with larger groups to celebrate the Sabbats and other special occasions. Whatever you call yourself comes down to choice - there is no right or wrong - and how you prefer to identify yourself. I prefer to be known as a witch, it describes well enough for me what I am and what I do and I'm lucky that my family, friends and work colleagues are sympathetic and understanding, many of my friends are witches themselves so I feel accepted for who and what I am but I have also had times when that was not the case.

Self-development is a common theme of all the branches of paganism and in practice this can mean anything from taking up Tai Chi, yoga or meditation to learning divination, aura balancing or healing. Witchcraft is very diverse and adaptable and welcomes these additions to the individual's faith. Many witches are employed in some kind of healing or spiritual practice, such as Reiki, crystal healing and herbalism as well as in more conventional healing careers like nursing or counselling.

The Sabbats are the eight festivals marking the changes of the seasons on what we call the Wheel of the Year. These are Imbolc on 1st February, Ostara at the spring equinox, Beltane on 1st May, Litha at the summer solstice, Lughnasadh (Lammas) on 1st August, Mabon or Madron at the autumnal equinox, Samhain on 31st October and Yule at the winter solstice. These festivals are celebrated by covens and solitaries alike and open rituals are often organised to which non-witches may be invited. These ceremonies honour and celebrate the abundant harvest, the first buds of spring, the beauty of the summer sun, the gathering together of families on long winter evenings.

Esbats are the monthly meetings held at the full moon. We give thanks to the goddess and god for all the things we are grateful for and carry out any healing or magic that has been asked for. Training, divination, healing circles or initiations are also carried out at the Esbat.

In addition to the Sabbats and Esbats, other important rituals for witches are birth, marriage and death. Wiccaning or naming ceremonies celebrate the birth of a baby. Sometimes a Goddess Mother and God Father, or Earth parents, the Pagan equivalent of Christian God parents, can be asked to look after the ongoing spiritual needs of the child in much the same way as a traditional god parent.

Although we may teach our children about Paganism and the craft and let them join in celebratory rituals, children in pagan families are encouraged to find out for themselves about different religions to decide which faith, if any, suits them. While children are not generally allowed to join a coven until the age of eighteen, depending on their interests and nature they can take part in open circles and family rituals. Anything involving journeys or quiet meditation will be far too boring for young children and so other events – such as pagan-oriented crafts or shorter rituals and plays – can be organised which will be more suitable for them. The children of pagans, druids, heathens and witches are free, like children of other faiths, to make up their own minds about what, if any, religion to follow as and when they are old enough to decide, though most of them find themselves quite at home with Paganism.

Hand-fasting is the old term used by Pagans for their wedding ceremonies. More often than not, these marriage partnerships are made legal by the addition of a civil service, although this is seen as secondary and irrelevant to the main ritual. The couple are literally joined together in love, with a ribbon loosely tying them together at the wrist – binding them together spiritually and physically. This is where the term 'tying the knot' comes from. The hand fasting cords are specially made for the couple and kept afterwards as a reminder of the promises made and the vows taken together. Jumping over a broomstick or fire for good luck and reciting sacred vows or poetry together are regular features of the ceremony which is performed by a priestess and/or priest. A hand-fasting can last for as long as the couple wish it; a year and a day is a common commitment for new love and leaves the couple free to separate after that time with no strings attached or to renew their vows if things went well; a life-time hand-fasting is for more dedicated couples who choose to remain together for the rest of their lives; another, deeper commitment to stay with each other throughout all of their incarnations is made by those who feel they have met their true soul-mate, someone they are destined to be with for lives beyond this one. There is a saying in the craft that when we meet our true soul-mate we will 'know and meet and remember and love them again.'

Although the death of a loved one can be a traumatic event for those left behind, we see it as a new beginning for those who have died. A Requiem service is held instead of the conventional church service and a lot of Pagans will choose a green burial site and wicker coffin. The requiem will usually include the breaking of a bowl and cutting of a silver cord to symbolise the life energy of the Beloved Dead being separated from the world of the living. Pagan ideas about death vary widely but generally we hold the belief that everyone lives on in spirit form after death and we are free to return to the world of the living through reincarnation or to remain in the spirit world, sometimes as a guide to the living. The Beloved Dead are honoured every year at Samhain with offerings at the altar.

A lot of people after learning about all of this still have that one question on their mind - does magic really work? If you have any real experience of witchcraft then you will know that the answer is yes, it does. If we have clear intentions and if the correct energy and concentration is put into it, magic does work. Healing magic is one of the most common requests for magic and most witches will cast spells to help their family and friends with other issues too, such as finding a new job or mending a broken heart.

Magic is a way of bending or shaping reality as it is now into the reality you want to exist. Underlying this is the concept of the web of life – the belief that we are all part of a universal energy and we are all connected. Magic works by clear visualisation and solid belief to send energy through the ether along the web of connections to affect changes in the physical world. Using magic effectively is the practice of seeing the current situation, visualising things the way you would prefer them to be and then manifesting this physically. Physicists have been able to show that this important magical concept can, to a certain extent, be scientifically verified – everything and everyone is made up of thousands of particles and these are the same, regardless of the form they make when they join together. You, the chair you sit on, the rain and the grass are all made up of the same energy. Quantum science has also shown that predictable results are not always so predictable after all and experiments, like Thomas Young's double-slit experiment with light waves and particles in 1820, have now been able to prove that just by observation we can change the behaviour of what we are observing. In the double-slit experiment, particles fired through a double-slit onto a target background were forming the interference pattern expected from waves, not the organised bands that particles should produce – the particles were behaving like waves. Under observation however, the particles produced the expected particle pattern – the very act of observing the experiment had changed the behaviour of the particles, an outcome which should have been impossible. Looked at from a witchy perspective, if we can change something by simple observation, imagine the possibilities for change when given concentrated focus and direction of energy!

Magic is the best word to describe our control over these energies right now and in the future, as science begins to explain the previously unexplained, perhaps that word will change.

Above all other considerations in working with energy and magic comes the Wiccan Rede. This phrase is widely recognised and acts as a guide line, laying down a code of ethics for making magic and spells.

> *Eight words the Wiccan Rede fulfil: An' it harm none, do what you will.*

The word *rede* means advice or counsel and this is the manner in which the phrase is used. Far from giving you the freedom to do exactly as you want, the rede stipulates that your actions shouldn't result in any kind of harm to anybody else. In practice, this means that when we do magic for whatever reason, we have at the very least asked permission of the person concerned and done our best to ensure that there are no negative intentions on their part or ours. It also means that when doing magic for ourselves, we are as sure as we can be that it is not going manipulate anyone else in the process of giving us the end result we're looking for. The way a spell is worded is certainly important, phrasing a chant in such a way that it cannot be misinterpreted for example, but as with every aspect of the craft, it is more important that the intention and focus of the spell are clear and positive rather than being selfish or wilfully harmful to others.

Be completely honest about it – do you really want to turn your ex-boyfriend into a toad or do you want to start afresh, start living your life again, moving forward with love and peace in your heart instead of those twisted feelings of hatred and vengeance? Do yourself a huge favour and let karma work its way on your ex!

Casting circles, invoking the elements, honouring the goddess and god, getting in touch with nature through the Wheel of the Year, raising energy for spells and healing, divination and celebratory rituals – all of these things are part of the witch's journey. When we gather in the presence of the Old Ones, we open ourselves to love, honesty and magic. There are so many things about the craft a novice wants to know, it's hard to know where to start and once the very basic elements of the craft have been conquered, and where does one go from there? What do we do once the circle has been cast and the elements invoked? How does witchcraft enter our everyday lives? What kind of practices can we learn?

There is no official text or bible from which all rituals, ceremonies or spells are taken. Likewise, there is no widely recognised consensus on the beliefs and practices of the craft as so much of it comes down to individual preference. There are some common threads running through the different styles of witchcraft; the observance of the eight Sabbats, the creating of sacred space, the belief in a goddess and god in some form, the reverence of nature and the ethical framework used with regards to spell casting and magic. There are several organisations which serve as advisory bodies and contact networks of Paganism in general and these can be a good starting point for anyone with a serious interest in the craft.

There are ways and means of finding out more advanced information, for example, getting in touch with covens or teachers through one of the numerous reputable pagan organisations, going to pagan-oriented café or pub moots, attending talks, workshops, camps and so forth. However, without that contact to the wider Pagan community, which is not for everyone, it can be difficult to get the knowledge, insights and teachings of the craft that lead to progress and development. Learning about witchcraft and all it encompasses can be a solitary and often lonely path. Of course, being a solitary witch is something many people are claiming as their chosen path and when it is the path of choice, the solitude and quietness are welcome, although many witches who join or form covens have started out on their own to begin with. For anyone without some links to a larger network when they want it, however, the solitary path can be harder to follow and there may be few or no opportunities for valuable interactions and discussions to share the experiences and meanings of the craft, especially if you live a remote area or don't have easy access to transport.

This book, therefore, is offered as a stepping-stone on the path of witchcraft, one that will guide you to the next level of understanding and practice. Circle casting, the five elements, invoking, consecration and magical associations have been covered in my previous book, *The Witching Path*, and in literally hundreds of other easily available books for beginners. There is a recap on these practices in the appendix, however, which will serve as a handy reminder if you need it.

I hope that this book will act as a spring-board, showing some of the interests and activities that can you study and develop once the foundations have built up. Don't take this all as gospel and do your own research into the topics suggested here that interest you as this is just the tip of the broomstick. The witch's journey is a long and winding path with many turns, tunnels, bridges and rope swings – spell casting, wand waving and velvet robes are not the be all and end all of witchcraft. Develop your spiritual path with your personal interests in mind, develop your understanding and experience and bring a sense sacredness, magic and empowerment into your everyday world.

CHAPTER 1

The Goddess and God

The goddess and god are equally venerated and honoured on the witching path with tributes, altars, offerings, poetry, chants and rituals dedicated to each. There is a perpetual love-story that binds them together and links in to the seasonal changes – you can do your own research and find your own tales of the god and goddess and how they interact but the bare bones of it go a little something like this: spring and early summer start them on the chase to become partners and lovers, both young and full of energy with the rising sun and the rutting season full upon them, as deer and stag they chase one another until finally he catches her and they mate in love; through later summer and autumn the goddess is pregnant, gaining maturity and wisdom and the god becomes the protector and hunter; winter sees the god going through a transformation in a fight to the death between the Holly King and the Oak King while the goddess is in her darker aspect, still heavily pregnant but also an elder who watches over the death that deep winter brings and finally, at the turn of the new year, she gives birth to the new King at the winter solstice, the Lord of the hunt is re-born so that he may grow and develop and come to chase her once more in the dance of love as the springtime earth re-awakens and she becomes again a young and desirable woman and so the cycle continues.

She is a goddess of the earth, a mother goddess, a virgin, a lover, friend, warrior, a blacksmith, a patron of poets and artisans, the one who gives birth to new souls, watches over their lives and then reaps them at the end of the cycle. She sits at the crossroads between life and death; she spins our threads, measures them and snips them off when we're done. She watches over childbirth, gives strength and energy to the crops we plant, she is the Mother. As the triple goddess of the moon, she goes from young woman to mature mother to aging crone; as a blacksmith, she forges magical weapons and as a hunter, she takes care of the animals of the forest, knowing the hunt depends on them thriving.

The goddess has been worshipped for thousands of years worldwide as a goddess of fertility, a mother goddess, sometimes a warrior, other times a healer or a poet. She is seen in the Sheila-na-gigs displayed in churches around the country and proudly, some would say vulgarly, displaying her genitalia for all to see while she grins wildly. She is honoured at temples across the world as in the Venus of Wilendorf; at Aqua Sulis in Bath a gilt bronze head of her as Sulis Minerva was discovered which is now on display in the museum. She is called Isis, Epona, Astarte, Diana, Brighid, Venus, Luna, Inanna, Gaia, Demeter, Cerridwen, Kali, Shiva, Mary, Yemaya, Lakshmi, Morrigan, Hecate and hundreds of other names. The goddess is the one we turn for guidance in matters of family, the heart, fertility of animals and crops, she is the mother of the earth and is also associated with the three phases of the moon.

As a young woman, virginal, pure, full of joy, vitality and life, the Maiden Goddess is tied in with the new and waxing moon. As a young woman, the goddess embodies fertility and growth - the moon is coming to life and growing in the sky again after its dark phase. The Maiden, then, is the aspect of the triple goddess we call on at a new moon ceremony for spells related to family, children, conception, growth, inspiration, creativity, seeking a new job or home, for planning and implementing new dreams, schemes and ideas. The mother goddess is seen as heavily pregnant, a mature woman, wiser and less impulsive than the maiden; the mother goddess watches over children and families and has the experience and wisdom of middle-age while still enjoying a life full of health and vigour. This phase is represented in the full moon when we can carry out magic for healing, manifesting our goals, making them solid and real; the mother's energy is comforting, consoling and never-ending. Rituals to help people deal with difficult situations and hard emotions are related to the full moon and the nurturing qualities of the mother goddess, as are spells for completion and manifestation. The third aspect of the goddess is the crone, an elderly woman with flowing white hair and a face full of deeply etched lines of worry and laughter – the crone is wise, knowledgeable and experienced and uses her insights to teach, advise and encourage us. The dark and waning moon link to the crone goddess. This is a time for letting things go and releasing old energies and spells can be done for getting rid of bad habits, banishing negative emotions like hatred and jealously, binding others from doing harm, dispelling what we no longer need.

Cerridwen, Epona and Brighid are the aspects of goddess I personally call on most often and there are many stories and myths surrounding them. You may wonder why I mention stories but bear with me; remember how much you looked forward to a story at bed-time as a child? They may have been just a story to us then but subconsciously we absorbed every word and now that we are adults we can understand the deeper levels of story and still enjoy them while learning the underlying themes and subtle depths of the tale. What we learn from the old stories, myths and legends will be slightly different for each of us but if we are prepared to think it through, to dig deeper into the minds of the characters, the influences, moods and morals of the tale, there is a great deal to be learned from story. The goddess story I love most and know the best is one of the tales of Cerridwen.

Cerridwen and her husband, Teggid Voel, have two children – Creirwy, the most beautiful girl in the world, and Afagddu, the ugliest boy in the world. Cerridwen decides that if her son cannot be handsome, then at the very least she can make him intelligent and wise and give him the gift of the Awen. And so she calls to the soul of the Awen and to the alchemist Pheryllts of Lake Bala and is given a recipe of herbs and roots that she must boil in a cauldron for a year and a day. When the brew is ready, just three drops of it will be enough to give her son enlightenment and intelligence beyond the worlds – but the remainder of the cauldron's potion will be poisonous. The goddess enlists the help of an old blind man, Morda, and a young boy, Gwion Bach, to stir the cauldron and tend its fire for the duration and the two of them do this quite happily, passing the long year with stories until eventually, the day arrives when the brew is finally ready. As Cerridwen approaches, however, the boy is startled and those precious three drops spill onto his skin. At once the goddess flies into a terrible rage, horrified that her poor Afagddu has lost out to this careless mortal wretch! She storms out to kill him but from the instant he instinctively sucked his burned finger and took the potion inside himself, Gwion was no longer an innocent – now he has the power of the Awen's magical brew running deep in his veins. He see the rage of the goddess and knows that she will kill him so changes at once into a hare and he runs. As a greyhound, Cerridwen gives chase and Gwion shifts to the form of a salmon and makes off in the river and as an otter, she races after him again. The salmon takes to the skies as a bird only to be chased again by Cerridwen who becomes a hawk and speeds after him. Gwion knows he cannot win the chase and he spies a pile of corn on the ground and there he sees his salvation, willing himself into the shape and form of a single grain. Cerridwen is not that easily fooled or defeated, however, she turns herself into a great black hen and eats every single ear and grain of the corn. Nine moons later, she gives birth to a son and she is still so full of hate that she can only think of killing the babe but on seeing his beauty, she sets him adrift in a river instead. Downstream and away, a fisherman pulls him to the riverbank and unwraps the swaddling, declaring the baby boy the most 'radiant brow' the world has ever known. The fisherman and his family take in the young boy, Taliesin, the radiant brow, and in time he grows up to become the greatest bard of all the land.

There are other tales of Cerridwen and many more of Taliesin but what I like about this story is how it shows the very deep and powerful love of a mother for her children; that beauty and love can overcome the vilest hatred; that the family we love are not necessarily born to us – displayed as the fisherman, Elphin, adopts the young Taliesin. Each element of the circle is invoked in the story – the fire of the cauldron, the salmon in water, the hare running over the earth and then the element of air when they goddess and boy fly as birds. As we connect to the elements in turn we are enriched with an understanding of them that at once enhances us spiritually and grounds us in reality. On another level, it's clear from the tale that we too can turn our negative emotions into love and forgiveness if we choose to view our situations in different ways and see the beauty inherent in all living things – no matter what the boy Gwion had done, the goddess – a woman grieving for what her own son has lost – was still able to forgive him and set him free. No matter how ugly her child, Cerridwen strives to help him and improve his situation – the positive aspects of our lives often get overshadowed by problems – money worries, ill health, arguments, poor relationships – when we sit back and take stock of the bigger picture we can find a way forwards, appreciate the things we do have and love others and ourselves despite our flaws.

Brighid again has many tales that take her through some wild adventures but as a personal aside to this, I just love the power and strength of Brighid as a blacksmith, typically a very male-dominated trade, yet here is she, a woman and a poet, stoking fiercely hot coals and wielding mighty hammers and transforming metal into swords, shields, axe-heads and jewellery. My sister is a blacksmith and it never ceases to amaze me that she can make a set of massive, heavy, wrought gates one day and the next a piece of delicate jewellery like the intricate oak-leaf pendant that she made at my husband's request as a hand-fasting gift.

Epona is a goddess of fertility who rides a white mare and is depicted across Europe in bas-reliefs and statues riding a horse, standing between two horses or lying on the back of a horse. Her Welsh equivalent is Rhiannon and Macha, or Emain Macha, is another horse goddess of the Celts. Her association with horses is important to me personally as the white horse is my totem animal and I was mad about horses as a young girl and rode as often as I could, spending every moment of my weekend at the local stables helping to muck out and clean tack just so that I could be close to the horses. The white horse chalk figures that dot the countryside, especially the Uffington horse, have always called to me and visiting sites like this that are associated with our deity can be a powerful and emotional experience.

The pagan god is the horned god of the forest; at once he is both the hunter and the stag who is being hunted. He is a father, a brother, a lover, a warrior, lustful and fun-loving, the wild, green man of the woods. He is consort to the great goddess, the powerful masculine force that drives us forwards. He is the joyful heart of celebrations, the silent watcher among the trees, the whisper of wind and the call of the wild. He is the wise old man offering guidance and the wisdom of experience. He is the all-seeing, all-knowing Father. Like the goddess, he has been given countless names; Ra, Apollo, Bran,

Odin, Pan, Cernunnos, Lugh, Zeus, Hades, Herne, Dionysus, Bacchus, Horus, Hotei, Loki, Osirs, Freyr, Thor and many more. The god is seen as having a dual-aspect with one being a young hunter and warrior, virile and lusty, the spirit of the woods while the other is an old wise man, a guide and elder, a white-bearded mentor with wisdom twinkling in his eyes.

The young God is often depicted with a weapon, a bow and arrows, a sword or hammer and he nearly always shows off his prowess with the ladies by sporting an erection, often out of all reasonable proportion. Priapus, the horned (and horny) god of Greek mythology had a permanently erect and incredibly large phallus. Son of Aphrodite and Dionysus, Priapus is a god of fertility and growth and also protector of shepherds and their flocks. Priapus presents an iconic image of the god across different cultures – where the goddess is depicted with large breasts and swollen belly, the god has his own fertility on show and so the duality of male/female is portrayed universally – from maypoles to a druid's staff or the handle of a witch's broom, the phallus is honoured and female genitalia and womb are seen in the chalice, the ribbons of red and white flowering around the maypole, the bristles that snuggly hold the staff of the broom. Interestingly, just as there is a representation of the Goddess, with the bronze head of Minerva, at the baths at Bath, there is also a statue of the God – a sun god thought to be associated with either Lugh or Apollo, complete with shining, sun-like rays coming from him like a crown of light. This is referred to by the museum there as the Gorgon but the gorgon was female and it was definitely snakes, not rays of sunlight, which adorned her hair. Another example of the pagan gods being honoured is the temple to Cernunnos beneath the cathedral of Notre Dame which was in use as late as the seventeenth century.

Pan is a well-known and popular god among pagans, the horny god who watches over shepherds and agriculture and plays his pipes in the high mountains, seducing the wood nymphs. The Dagda is a god whose name means the 'good god' and he is full of sexual potency, strength, abundance, a fearsome warrior with a huge club that took nine mortal men to lift and that would slay nine men with a single blow, Dagda was the father and king figure of the Tuatha de Danann (people of the goddess Danu who retreated to live as the Sidhe, the faerie folk in the hills of Ireland after their defeat by the Gaels). Tales of the Dagda include feats of endurance, challenges of eating or drinking impossible amounts and often there's an element of humour as he makes a bit of a fool of himself yet still manages to best his challengers. Cernunnos, closely associated with Herne the hunter, is a horned god of Celtic mythology seen in rock carvings, stone carvings and statues and, of course, on the famous Gundestrup cauldron. Again, a god of obvious fertility and deeply involved with the creatures of the land, he is especially linked to deer and snakes who is he often pictured with, sometimes the snake is coiled around his staff or neck and he wears stag or deer antlers on his head. The name Herne/Cernunnos is an hh–rr–nn sound or k-rr-nn sound reminiscent of the deep, low calling of a stag and let's think for a moment of the Cerne Abbas giant, the chalk figure of Dorset, who is another blatant honouring of male fecundity. Herne, however is not really a god despite the fact that a lot of pagans use his name in their rituals, rather, he is a figure of folklore who is said to ride across Great Windsor Park, leading the wild hunt in times of national tragedy.

We can plainly see that these ithyphallic gods represent masculine fertility of the land and animals. The flip-side of this is the father figure, the elder, leader and wise man. The winter god is a wise old one, he has wisdom, insight, intelligence, experience, knowledge and the gift of divination – as seen in Oghma, who gave us the Ogham oracle and Odin, who gave us runes. Twice every year the cycle of the god and the cycle of the sun gives us the battle of young over old, innocence over wisdom, in the fight between the Oak King and the Holly

King. At the winter solstice the mantle of leadership is won by the Oak King and at mid-summer solstice the Holly King takes the crown. The battle scene, often acted out in covens with a dramatic flair, takes place in part to remind us of the balance we need in our lives between impulsive actions and well-laid plans, rash decisions and focused thought, the balance between young and old – naivety and wisdom, inspiration and completion. Where the young man will dash out to seek revenge or justice, the old man will sit back on his haunches, listen to all sides and make an impartial and fair judgement based on long experience and knowledge. I think of the old god as a healthy old hermit, living simply off the land, to whom we can turn, not just for the advice we want but also, and more importantly, for the advice we don't want to hear.

Here's another story, a tale of the Dagda, the 'good god', a somewhat plain and ordinary persona wrapped around mighty strength and masculine potency. The Tuatha De Danann's enemies were the Fomors who they had once defeated and who they were about to face again. The Dagda approached the Formors on a spying mission under pretence of talking about a possible truce. The Fomors, knowing about the Dagda's love of porridge and great feats of endurance, set before him a vast amount of porridge – eighty cauldrons in one version and a whole pitfull in another – and challenged him to eat it all if he could. Of course, the Dagda ate the whole lot and asked for more. The Fomors laid out huge cauldrons filled milk, fat, oatmeal with added sheep and pigs and once again, the Dagda consumed it all. So impressed with his endurance and his smooth-talk, one of the Formorian women was completely won over and seduced. She was even more in awe of him once he had impressed her with his skilful love-making. The Dagda's lover was so taken with him that she vowed to turn her magic against her own people, helping the Tuatha De Danann in the forthcoming battle. Impressive indeed!

As it was with tales of the goddess, so it is with tales of the god – in his myths we see the truths that we can apply to our lives. Endurance and persistence are just as important to our growth and development, both spiritual and physical, as are good health and strength. As we saw in the tale of Cerridwen, love can overcome prejudice. We also learn from this that not everybody is who they seem to be – after all, in this story it is the Dagda himself who is hiding behind a façade of truce while underlying it he plots and schemes for his own ends. We must give our trust wisely or risk being hurt but give it we must or we are left without knowing the value of it. If this god seems irrelevant to you, then pay honour to one who rings true in your soul.

We should not follow blindly what we have been told with regards to the Old Ones – far better to honour and respect a deity who means something to you - study them, read up and do your homework. Find out the old stories and legends of the Old Ones, think about how you can relate their adventures and aspects to your own life, delve into the mystery of your story, invite and welcome in the aspects of divinity that you need in your life to help you grow, develop, embrace, let go and move forward.

Journey Time

Try this guided journey or something similar but along these lines to start with to give yourself a way of connecting to and understanding more about the goddess and god. This book assumes you have basic experience of relaxation and visualisation techniques but if you lack that, don't worry about it for now as we'll go into more detail on this deep kind of journey work later and you can come back to this exercise at any time. Start out small and build up over the weeks, months and even years, to carry out longer and more detailed visions and journeys – this relationship, harmony and understanding of deity is not something you will ever stop needing. Your learning, growth and development will never end and your connection to the goddess and god will diminish and weaken if you don't make time for it in your life.

You can choose to do this with others or alone, outdoors or inside, at night or daytime. Pick a place and time where you won't be interrupted and have ready anything you might want in your circle; book of shadows, candles, incense, your wand or athame, cushions to keep your comfy, something you can burn or bury as an offering afterwards. Make sure you'll be warm enough and put a glass of water and an apple on the altar. There is a short chakra exercise first that you can try as a way of both opening the chakras and reaching a deeply relaxed state of mind. Get into the habit of doing this kind of meditative relaxation often; the benefits of it are enormous even without the journey work.

Create your sacred space by casting a circle and do your invocations as normal and then prepare for the journey by lying down comfortably. Relax as fully as you can. Close your eyes.

Breathe deeply. Breathe. Be still, be silent. Silence your thoughts and relax more deeply. Visualise each of your chakras opening in turn and let the colours of the chakra wash over you in soothing light. Opening the chakras also increases our connections to spiritual power and energy. Use the chakra exercise below to enhance and deepen your state of openness and relaxation and spend enough time on each chakra individually to really feel its pulsating, colourful, energy.

Focus clearly on the energy of your Root chakra. See it as red, a sparkling, pulsing energy, getting bigger and more powerful the more you focus on it. Breathing deeply, breathing energy into the chakra with each breath. Feel the root chakra become stronger until it begins to spiral upwards to the next chakra. See the energy flowing from the root and up into your sacral chakra next. An orange vortex of energy, gradually spinning faster and growing bigger, sending the limitless energy up to the next level. Your solar plexus chakra, yellow and vibrant, begins to enlarge next, swelling and spiralling. See the energy coming up through the root and sacral chakras into this one, expanding the yellow vortex and making it grow and then pass energy up along the spiral thread to the next chakra. The green heart chakra begins to expand now, energy still coming up from the lower chakras. See it getting bigger and stronger and feel the energy as it surges upwards. Your throat chakra now fills up and becomes a spinning, swirling ball of blue energy, growing and energising you, it fills up to capacity and this blue energy begins to go up the thread again. The lower chakras are still sending more energy up along the central, spiralling thread, now feeding your third eye, or brow, chakra. The violet light of the brow centre grows and spirals, larger and brighter and gives energy up to the next chakra.

As your energy spirals up to the crown chakra, right on top of your head, visualise all the colours of each chakra coming up to the white chakra at your crown, whooshing out above you and then cascading down around you to bathe and fill up your aura.

You are now completely relaxed and at peace. Visualise yourself in a small wooded area, somewhere familiar to you where you feel comfortable and safe. The sky is clear and blue and the sun gently warms your skin. The sounds of rustling leaves and bird song come to you. Be aware of how peaceful and calm the surroundings are making you feel. Ahead of you, a tall, broad tree stands out from the rest. Head towards it, noticing what a giant of a tree it is, with gnarly bark and branches jutting out like swooping arms at all angles. As you get closer to the tree, notice how the bark is cracked and split and seems to open up like a crevice. A darkness from inside that crevice calls you forwards, drawing you in. Close enough to touch the tree now, you realise you can fit inside this opening. Take a moment before entering the body of the tree to centre yourself, take a deep breath and ask: *Am I ready to see the goddess? Am I ready to meet with the gods?* If not, then it's okay to leave the tree, close down your chakras and try again some other time.

If you're happy to, then go ahead and clamber in through the opening, away from the light of the sunny woods and the chirruping birds, right into the belly of the tree where it is dark and littered with cobwebs. It is very quiet inside the tree and so dark you can only just make out in front of you a narrow, winding stairwell that leads downwards. Follow it, feeling your way down with your hands on the solid wall of wood that surrounds you. A rope of red, black and white, acts as a guide and it seems that there is no end to these spiralling steps but eventually a light begins to glow softly from below and gradually it brightens. You reach solid ground under your feet and there is a small fire in the centre of a cavern. The light of the fire doesn't illuminate much but you can see there are further openings on either side of the cavern. Sit or stand by the fire and ask for the god and goddess to come and meet you. As they appear either together or one at a time, take notice of their appearance. Are they old, young, dressed in finery, wearing armour or accompanied by animals? Do they fit your expectations? Introduce yourself, say hello and thank them for meeting with you. You might want to explain why you have done this journey, ask questions, ask for guidance. Find out if there is anything you need to know from them in order to move forwards with your path. See if they have any requests of you, any offering they would like to receive or any spiritual work you should be doing. Spend as long as you like talking with the god and goddess, there is no right or wrong thing to say or do.

When you feel it's time to leave, give your thanks, remember any promises of offerings you've made and say farewell. Turning away from the fire, you come again to the steps that wind upwards now, getting darker as you leave the cavern. The wooden walls and the rope guide you back up the trunk of the great tree and although it seems like a long climb, you eventually see daylight. Squeeze out of the crack in the tree bark and back into the glade. Is it still a beautiful day? Has it become cloudy? Has time moved on towards dusk? Are the birds still singing as they were before? Step right away from the tree and then look back to face it a final time. Say thank you. Say farewell. Gradually become aware of your surroundings in the real world. Feel the weight of your body; breathe; be aware of where you are now in the physical world once more.

Close your chakras down by reversing the process you did at the start, all except the crown chakra which always remains slightly opened. See clearly your chakras slowly unwinding, closing like a flower closes at the end of the day, the vibrating colours winding down the body from one chakra to the next, from crown to brow, to throat to heart, solar plexus to sacral and finally to the root chakra at the base of your spine.

Be aware of your breathing, the feel of clothes against your skin, everyday sounds and sensations. Keep your eyes closed for a few minutes until you feel ready to face the mundane world again. There's no hurry; the process takes as long as it takes. Open your eyes, slowly sit up and breathe deeply once or twice, clap your hands, tap the floor or whatever else it is that you do to ground yourself after visualisation. Have something to eat and drink, make notes on your experience in your book of shadows. If you didn't feel right doing this exercise today or if you didn't gain anything from it you can try it again any time you want to. There's no right or wrong, no have-to or should.

Invoking

Invoking the god and goddess into a circle is done as a matter of course in most pagan groups and goes along these lines: *I do hereby invoke and welcome the goddess, Isis, into the circle, lend your power unto our spells and* … and there's nothing wrong with that provided that the invocation is felt, honoured, understood and respected by everyone in the group. Everybody present should offer their own energy as the invocations take place; with thirteen or so people concentrating on the god and goddess, a much stronger essence and spirit of the divine will be called into the circle.

Invocations to the earth, spirit, air, goddess etc., should be spoken out loudly and proudly, while internally bringing to mind your connection and the emotions and feelings involved with that element/deity and your relationship with it. If we cannot truly feel earth in our heart and soul, we cannot truly bring it into being in the circle between the worlds. When you call out your invocation to the Old Ones, do it with feeling, do it with meaning.

Drawing down the moon is a way of deeply connecting to the goddess energy, of pulling that feminine divine spark down into yourself so that you become the physical embodiment of the goddess. Done at Sabbats or the full moon esbat, the Priestess carries out the ritual with the aid of her coven Priest. While there is no real reason why you cannot do this by yourself, a coven has its merits in terms of offering support and guidance and is a good way to carry out the ritual. The aim of this rite is to give the Priestess extra insight and a deeper level of connection with the specific goddess she is embodying; to act as a medium for the goddess to speak with information, prophecies or knowledge for the coven and also to allow the goddess to add blessings and power to spell casting, divination and ritual.

In some cases, the goddess persona completely takes over the Priestess, who may have no recall of the event or what she said and how she acted during the process. Most of the time, however, the Priestess retains her knowledge and control over her actions as the goddess enters her, speaks through her and guides her. Some women feel energised and more fully alive, others might be in more of a trance-state, and some will feel acutely aware of their surroundings and their connections to nature. Make sure you are familiar with the aspects and traits of the goddess you are calling on if you are drawing down a specific goddess.

If you do this yourself or are assisted through it as part of a coven, you, as priestess, take on the qualities and essence of the goddess. In a group situation, the main assistant, normally the priest, will need to keep a close eye on the priestess – it can be a draining process if it goes on for a long time, especially if she is raising and directing energy for magic as well as being aware of the presence of the goddess within her. Before carrying out the ritual, the Priestess would be wise to delegate a specific person who will act as her watcher, to ensure that if she becomes too spaced out, too taken over or has any other physical or psychological effects, there will be someone on hand who can politely ask the goddess to leave the physical vessel. The Priest or another watcher/guardian must also make sure that the Priestess is fully grounded after the ritual and generally look after her if she needs it and take over closing the ritual if necessary.

Usually a woman embodies the goddess and a man embodies the god in the rite of Drawing Down the Sun, but as we are all part of everyone and everything, inextricably linked, there is no real reason why this should always be the case.

Create a sacred space using a smudge bundle or a bell to cleanse the ritual area and then cleanse everyone who is going to take part in the ritual. It is best done in view of the full moon and out of doors if you can. Cast the magic circle in your usual way, calling on the five elements to be present and witness the ritual.

Invocations to the Goddess

Stand upright with your arms raised outwards and upwards and begin to invoke the goddess to come into you. In a group, your assistant will carry out the invocation for you, adjusting the words if necessary. There are literally hundreds of goddess invocations in various Wiccan texts books and on the internet, this is one I have written and used with success; you can make up your own or use this one or another. As you recite the invocation, raise your arms high and start to lower them slowly, as you begin to sense the goddess energy descending into you. If you want to embody a particular goddess, use her name in the invocation.

Goddess of the moon, Maiden, Mother and Crone,
I invoke you, Ancient Goddess, hear my call,
Come, Goddess, come; into this Priestess, your physical vessel.
Be present, Lady of the old ways.
By root and bud, by leaf and flower,
By moon and sun, by night and day,
So do I ask you, in love and trust,
To come, Goddess, come.

If you do sense that the goddess has come into you then welcome her. It is customary for anyone present to also welcome the goddess, usually by reciting poetry dedicated to her in the form of the evocative Charge of the Goddess as written by Doreen Valiente or something similar to it - you can make up your own poem or charge in honour of her or use the one I've written here.

I am the Great Goddess, the creator of the world, the maker of magic, and the lover of Man. I am She who lets all things live, who fills all creatures with life and love and laughter, with warmth and comfort and knowledge and wisdom. I am she who sends forth all life unto the earth with joy and love and trust. I am the Death Mother to whom all creatures return and I welcome them with open arms. I stand apart from time and creation, for I am the light beyond the edge of darkness against whom time has no measure. I am the Mother, the Daughter, the Sister, the Lover, the Huntress, the Prophetess and the Keeper of Dreams. I am she who watches over the world. All things are sacred to me and all things are part of me. Let all who honour me be blessed by my light, for behold, I am the Great Goddess.

Following this part of the rite, you might like to perform magic and divination or to carry out any cleansings, blessings and consecrations in the name of the goddess and direct the energy raised by yourself and/or the group. In coven situations, the other coven members are to treat their priestess with respect and courtesy and can use the opportunity to ask for guidance and help with problems or to make offerings to the goddess.

After carrying out the rest of your ritual and before you start to close the circle, you should give thanks to the goddess for her presence. Acknowledge any special help she has given you, any insights you have received and ask for her blessings as she leaves.

I give my thanks to you, Great Goddess of the moon, for the wisdom and power you have given to me. In honour, love and trust, I ask you to depart and bid you return to your realms. Hale and farewell.

You should now give thanks to the Horned God and the elements as normal and close the circle.

You can adapt the ritual above to drawn down the god in one of his many guises. The following invocation and declamation can be used instead, substituting the name of Cernunnos for the god you identify with. As with before, the aim of the rite is to connect to and understand the aspects of the god you're invoking and to allow insights and wisdom to come through for the rest of the coven and yourself. Be sure to finish off with an offering and thanks.

Invocations to the God

God of the forest, God of the mountain,
I invoke you now to hear my call,
Come, Cernunnos, come; into this Priest, your physical vessel.
Be present, Lord of the old ways.

By crown and antler, by horn and staff,
By shining sun and raven wise,
So do I ask you, in love and trust,
To come, Cernunnos, come.

I am the Lord of the Forest, I am Herne the Hunter and Pan of the wilds, I am He who is forever present, forever virile and forever within your soul. I am He who is the heat of sun, the heart of love, the rutting stag and the hunting green man. Consort of the Great Goddess, I hold all wild, unknown things in my sway, I give my strength to the corn in the fields and the eagle that soars – I am the prey upon which I prey. I am the salmon in the weir, I am the rising sap, I am the raven in the sky and the sun that guides your day. I am the Father of all, I am the wise man at the edge of the world, between the worlds and within your soul. I am that masculine force that you forever seek and I have been with you since the beginning and I am there as you reach the end. I am the dread lord of the underworld, the green king of holly and oak and all things and all souls are sacred to me. Let all who honour me be blessed by my light for behold; I am the God of the Wilds.

I give my thanks to you, oh God of the holly and oak, for the wisdom and power you have given to me. In honour, love and trust, I ask you to depart and bid you return to your realms. Hale and farewell.

CHAPTER 2

The Wheel of the Year

The eight festivals we celebrate as pagans and witches, druids and heathens, revolve around the seasons of the year, the cycles of the sun, the phases of life from birth to maturity, to old age and death. There is no beginning and there is no end, one phase leads right through to the next and with each passing phase we lose something of the old and gain something of the new. Each Sabbat is awash with folklore, traditions and customs that you can research and introduce into your practice along with seasonal themes, colours, foods and recipes. Some of the best ways to celebrate the Sabbats include a big feast and party with themed decorations and activities, like carving a pumpkin for Samhain, looking out for snow drops at Imbolc and kissing under the mistletoe at Yule.

I feel that not only does the cycle of the Sabbats follow the seasons but each season and festival corresponds with the elements too, with the cycles of life and re-birth - even on a daily basis we pass from one state of being to the next, constantly evolving and moving forward. It is not a linear journey but if any one Sabbat calls out to me as the starting point of the year, it has to be Imbolc so that's where I shall start now with this forewarning: please don't expect a pre-written, prescriptive ritual to follow for each Sabbat, or indeed any ritual in this book. I've included ritual poems for one sabbat, recipes and activities for another but in order to truly progress and develop on your witching journey, you really will benefit from making up your own poems, chants, rituals and ceremonies. This is more of a melting pot of ideas for those who already know and understand the basics rather than a 'how-to' for beginners. Our rituals and celebrations tend to have the same formats so you can pick up on the ideas included here and use these to create your rituals – you can dip into this to find the underlying themes of each Sabbat along with different ways of celebrating that can be applied and adapted for any festival or ritual. The appendix contains the format and ritual structure to keep as your basic template for the Sabbats and any other rituals and spell workings and take this brief sojourn through the wheel of the year as an inspiration to uncover the rest of the journey.

Imbolc/Imbolg

1st February, a fixed Sabbat and a fire festival, the first of the two spring festivals.

This time of year is full of promise – hard frosts and snow on the ground harden some of the bulbs and seeds that have been planted and forces them up through the ground. Shoots of snowdrops and the first hints of greenery on the trees and bushes spring into tentative life. Spring lambs are well on the way, some of them already born by now, giving the name 'Oimelc', meaning ewe's milk, to the festival. The cold and biting winds and the rains and snow are interspersed with bright sunshine that rises earlier and earlier each day as we head towards spring. Imbolc is a season of anticipation and excitement – are the daffodils starting to shoot yet? Will the lambs be born healthy? Shall we have a deep snow this year or not? Often it is the coldest time too, and I love the winter woollies that people don - so often without realising it, we choose brightly coloured scarves and hats that highlight the colours of flowers that are just around the corner.

The Christian festival of Candlemass is also held on February 1st and yes, perhaps that was a deliberate ploy of the early Christian faith to win over Pagans who weren't prepared to give up a celebration on that day but I know a few Pagans who use this name for Imbolc. It embodies that sense of returning light – a mass of candles, bringing them into a sacred place to be blessed, people coming together as a community to honour light and warmth.

In agricultural areas the land is being prepared, ploughed and turned over ready for planting and sowing. Imbolc literally means 'ewe's milk' and the festival is so named with good reason for a visit to any farm at this time of year will attest to the fact that sheep who were mated the previous year are now bearing their young and there are frisky lambs aplenty. As well as sheep, many other animals have their young at this time of year and that includes us human animals too. Babies conceived at Beltane will be born around Imbolc. For centuries people have honoured the goddess Bride or Brighid at Imbolc and as pagans and witches today we still carry out some of the original traditions with a little bed made up for Bride in the centre of the circle. She is represented as a doll dressed in white and welcomed in, sometimes little 'gifts' are given though this could be as simple as giving her an offering of incense, food and drink.

Imbolc is the preferred time for witch initiations as it strongly associated with new beginnings so the majority of witches, both groups and solitaries, will wait until Imbolc to hold initiations and dedications. Rituals for Imbolc normally involve plenty of candles, lit in honour of the returning light and usually the goddess, as Brighid or Bride, is welcomed as above. She is a Celtic goddess of the hearth, a blacksmith and poet, a warrior, healer and midwife. With so many powerful attributes, Brighid is a useful goddess to call on for many reasons and combined with the birthing season of Imbolc and the promise of warmer, easier times ahead, Imbolc can be a powerful time for magic.

Group rituals for Imbolc often have people calling out in the circle what they want to achieve and work towards over the coming year and then collecting a packet of seeds to plant – the idea being that as your seeds grow, so will your goals. Small toys of fluffy white lambs, a glass of milk or a vase of snowdrops can go on the altar. Swap ideas and plans, plant a piece of paper with your plans on it under your seeds and let it germinate. There are plenty of other things that could be done for Imbolc, too. It's one of the four fire festivals so instead of burying your wishes you could ask people to write their goals on paper which is then burned in the fire, releasing the energy raised as the smoke rises. Thoughts for the coming year could be written on a slip of paper and placed inside a white helium balloon to be released into the sky, taking the wish and your energy up to the air elementals, ready to be worked on and then brought back down to you when it's ready.

Spells for Imbolc include working towards to a new job or promotion, fertility magic, spells for children and animals and magic for a new beginning, making plans and designing dreams for a better, brighter future. Decide ahead of time what you want to work for – new home, new relationship, starting to work towards your dreams – and plan your ritual around that. Collect things that represent your ideas – feathers, plants, pebbles, twigs, little toy houses, seeds, candles with inspirational shapes or colours, photographs or poems – and create a ritual that is all about bringing things into being and making a start on your plans in the real world.

Ostara

22nd March, depending on the astronomical timing, is the day of the spring, or vernal, equinox and the druid festival of Alban Elir. The days and nights are of equal length and from now on the days will get longer and the weather (we hope) will get warmer and the late nights and early mornings are getting lighter every day from now on until we reach the solstice.

Hear me, I am the budding leaf and rooting tree.
Hear my call in the winds, blowing away the web of cold winter.
Hear me as I awaken, the great mother earth rising anew.
Hear me, I am the balance of day and night,
Feel the kiss of my warmth upon your skin, feel me settle deep within.

The Ostara Sabbat is another festival that has a Christian equivalent as Easter, though Easter and Ostara rarely, if ever, fall on the same day, with the Christian celebration normally a few weeks later. In my family we celebrate Ostara at the equinox with chocolate eggs, painted or dyed hen's eggs and daffodils on the altar. So that we don't miss out on the very nice tradition of easter eggs, we also have what I refer to as Chocolate Egg Day! Chocolate eggs as a religious symbol never had any real meaning for me as a child and the idea of an easter rabbit delivering eggs, a concept that wasn't around in the UK when I was young, is even odder and sits uncomfortably in my mind. One explanation posed for the easter bunny are tales of ground nesting birds temporarily leaving their nice warm eggs in a shallow dip while on the hunt for food – along comes Brer Rabbit who finds a good spot to lie down for a while and is startled into running off at the slightest noise of the returning bird; thus it appears that as the rabbit or hare darts away from his resting place, he leaves behind a clutch of eggs! We can't possibly talk of Ostara and eggs without mentioning the tradition of blowing the insides out of an egg shell, putting a ribbon through and painting and decorating the eggs as an altar decoration. Children and adults love this but rubber or foam eggs from a craft shop might be more suitable for tiny hands.

The annual spring clean of my grandmother's era is a tradition that has merit. As we shuffle off the final throes of frosty Imbolc and see warmth and light return to our homes, we sweep away all the debris, physical and psychological, of the previous year to leave the house clean, fresh and ready to welcome in better times. The big clean must be done before the end of May to avoid bad luck and if any soot should fall on you while sweeping the hearth, it indicates that money is on its way, though how many of us have a real hearth now? Despite the phobia many people have developed of spiders and cobwebs, spiders are actually a symbol of good luck and if you sweep out a spider's web you must first ask permission of the spider so it is forewarned and can find a new place to live – if you don't ask first, the spider will bring you bad luck.

As well as continuing the custom of spring cleaning and egg-giving, we celebrate the spring equinox with a ritual Sabbat for Ostara to mark the change in season and give blessings to the new beginnings and projects that are now underway. The altar is decorated with brightly coloured cloths, a vase of daffodils, painted eggs, statues and pictures of the goddess as the blossoming Maid of spring. That much loved symbol of rural spring time, the gambolling lamb, can be represented on the altar too in the form of a photograph or postcard, as a sign of the joy and vitality that spring brings to us.

The Ostara ritual is based on the theme of awakening – letting go of the old to make room for the new and planting the seeds of new ideas. This might mean selling your car in order to make way for one which is in better condition or it might be realising that a particular dream or goal is no longer what you want to aim for and choosing something else to aspire to instead. New dreams, goals, aspirations, new friendships, you name it - whatever there is in your life and whatever you wish to come into it, there is always room for expansion and spring is the ideal time to make way for it.

For a solitary Ostara ritual fill your altar with things like incense, bells, singing bowls, a vial of consecrated salt water, rattles, a drum, whistles, smudge sticks, feathers and anything else that can be used for cleansing – physically as well as psychically. Take up your cleansing tools and go methodically around the whole of the house – outside too if possible.

Smudge the windows and doors, the corners of each room. Chime a bell or shake a rattle to dust away the influences of the previous year. Use your besom to brush away dust and sweep away dirt and when the house is clean and its energy refreshed, start working on your aura. Use smudge and feathers to cleanse your energy and bless yourself with a consecrated salt and water mixture and then take time to do a tree-of-life grounding meditation – roots down, shoots up, connecting deeply to that universal energy that is pure love and honesty. Seal your aura with a protective barrier of gold or silver light (see chapter five for more on the aura).

Wish Bird

Both Imbolc and Ostara have their specific traditions as we have seen and the two festivals are quite different in their feeling, Imbolc still full of frost and promise while Ostara has already started to fulfil that promise and the weather, and our general mood with it, has improved. However, both of these celebrations relate to the element of air, the childhood cycle of life, dreams and inspirations, all things which are not necessarily tangible. Air is the element of new beginnings, dawn, dreams, the starting point of a journey, so it's a good element to use at the starting point of the year too. Try this gentle energy working to create a powerful and vibrant bird form that can carry your dreams, goals and aspirations off onto the web of wyrd to be transformed and brought back to you in a different form.

As part of your festival celebrations or at another time during the Imbolc-Ostara season, and preferably on the evening of a new moon, stand still and be silent. You should be in a circle, cleansed thoroughly, grounded and with your chakras opened. Do not speak or whisper a word while you create this ethereal bird. Close your eyes. Bring your palms together and activate the chakras in your palms by rubbing them against each other as if warming your hands on a cold day. Rub vigorously then pull your hands apart, palms facing each other. You should feel the tingle of energy, buzzing lightly between your hands. If you feel nothing or if the energy spot you have raised is weak, keep working at it. When you feel that warm glow, that magnet-like barrier of energy in your hands, turn your attention to your root chakra and feel your connection through it to the ground, deep into the core of the earth. Pull gently on the line of power that anchors you there and draw energy up through your roots and into your body, up through the lower chakras and out through your palms to join with and expand the energy ball you already have. And now go higher, to your crown chakra. Put one hand high up and open yourself to the spirits of air, the clouds, the heavens and stars. Pull on this channel of energy and bring it gently down towards you, through your palm, into your arm and through your crown chakra, further down. Let it come through your hands and add to the energy that is gathering.

Keep pulling up from the earth and down from the sky, physically and psychically, to press all that energy into the ball form between your hands, let it grow and grow. When it reaches a decent size, say as big as a watermelon, use both hands to squash it smaller, get it to condense right down into a much smaller, tomato-sized ball of concentrated energy. By now it should be bubbling and fizzing with charge. Once more draw energy into it from the earth and sky, from moon and stars, from air and water, fire and earth, let it grow again as you add more energy to it. When you have something about as big as a bird – it could be any bird, a robin, a hawk, a pigeon, an eagle, a buzzard or a heron – stop calling more energy in and begin to shape it. Open your eyes so you can see what you're doing and hold the wish bird with your hands, patting the energy into place, shaping it, smoothing it, giving it wings and a head, a tail, legs. Carve this energy gently to form your bird and let it rest in your hands. Now bring your wish to mind – what do you want to begin? Hold this thought clearly and bring the bird up to your face and whisper your wish to the energy form you've created. Tell the wish bird what you desire, what you wish for.

Hold still for just a second, really focused and concentrated and then – lift your hands up to the skies and let the bird fly free. Let it soar away, flying out of view and out of reach, into the sky, into the air. Let it go and let your wish go with it. Give thanks and close your circle, make an offering and know that your wish bird is carrying your wishes on the air to the places it needs to go to be fulfilled.

Beltane

1st May, a fixed date. Beltane is the beginning of real warmth and we have usually had our first taste of the hot sun by now. Maypoles – and their phallic symbolism – are still seen today and it's a true pleasure to dance beneath them, winding the red and white ribbons around the pole. Done properly, the ribbons are circled in different ways to create a wide range of patterns as the dancers weave in and out of each other, over and round and under.

The May Queen or Queen of the May, and sometimes a May King, are chosen and paraded through the villages on floats and the mummers plays of ancient custom are still carried out here and there, such as the ones at Padstow and Abbots Bromley or the morris dancing that we see across the width and breadth of the UK. May day marks the start of the rutting season of nature when the god and goddess, as hind and stag, run and leap and chase through the forest in the dance of love and lust and that theme of love, lust, passion and sexy chase is echoed in the old saying of May day – *hurray, hurray for the first of May, outdoor sex begins today!*

So there in a nutshell is the over-riding theme of Beltane. Make merry while the sun is shining and enjoy the gift of warmth, the gift of your body and enjoy being with the ones you love. One other theme of Beltane for me on a personal note is that as a family we are spending much more time outside and enjoying the great outdoors with the first big camp of the year on the closest weekend to Beltane. Usually with a group of family and/or friends, we normally end up in the peak district for a few days and have a woodland ritual around some of the ancient standing stones in the area. So as well as the sexiness of the season, the warmth and activities going on, we are truly connecting on a very real level with nature once more.

The Beltane ritual can revolve around an upright staff, a tree, a maypole if you have access to one. If not, dig your staff into the ground and tie red and white ribbons at the top or at least put something in the centre of your space, even if it's just a pot-plant – though the more phallic the item at your centre the better! Dance and weave and chase around it, winding ribbons, casting your magic into the dance with a chant that matches your aims. If you are trying to conceive then why not visit a local standing stone for the great rite? If there aren't any close to where you live, you can at least erect the ancient altar and enjoy yourselves in some natural place out of doors where you can be undisturbed for a while.

Beltane is the season of blossoming love and a perfect time for hand-fastings. The binding of two souls for a year and a day or for all of this life or for this life and all of those beyond… A hand fasting ritual, I believe, should be written specially for each couple and never used again. Provided it is planned in advance, it's nice to be able to include pagan friends of the couple to call in the quarters or to bind the cords around their wrists. The essence of the hand fasting is to join them, symbolically and actually – exchanging vows and tying the wrists together is just a small part of the ceremony. Some couples finish off with jumping over a low fire or a broomstick to symbolise leaving their old lives behind, getting rid of what once was before starting life together anew – though if you're ready to commit yourself to someone, shouldn't you have got rid of your baggage already by this stage? Hand fasting rituals have an element of seriousness about them too – the couple are asked a series of questions that convinces themselves, one another, the priest/ess and the gathered onlookers, of the serious nature, honesty and integrity of this commitment. They swear on the powers of earth, air, fire, water and spirit that they will keep their vows.

Hand fasting cords for a couple should be similarly unique and made specifically - I'm fairly adept at textile crafts so I will knit a long cord of organic wool and bind it with ribbons and strips of cloth in their favourite colours – perhaps a snippet of the bride's dress fabric or a button that matches the grooms waistcoat. Little charms and tiny pendants that represent the couple's interests are woven into the cords. If either of the couple have children they can be included too, if circumstances allow. Children can be given a small gift as a token of their place in the family and the couple's commitment to them as well as to each other. Teens might want to invoke one of the quarters and younger children or babies can be held and honoured during the ceremony. Once more with the theme of Beltane and the love and warmth of a heart-felt ceremony we see the honesty, playfulness and uniqueness of paganism – the joy of being free to choose how we celebrate and what is included while still having the guidelines and experience of those who have gone before to show us the way.

Litha

20th – 22nd June depending on the actual day of the summer solstice, this is the druid festival of Alban Hefin. We celebrate Litha to honour the longest day of the year, the height of the sun god's power, knowing that although the days will shorten from now on until the winter solstice, we have the best of the year's weather still ahead of us. Summer is full of barbeques, parties, sun-bathing, holidays with people we love, dancing, merriment, late nights and sultry days, brightly coloured clothes, picnics, ball games in the park and the simple enjoyment of a lazy country walk on a gorgeous day. Summer is a vibrant, busy time of year and agriculturally the sun, at its most prominent position in the sky, is aiding the growth of crops. We celebrate the solstice by staying up through the night to see the sunrise on midsummer's day either with our working groups, on our own, or by joining one of the huge public rituals at places like Stonehenge and Avebury, honouring the sun by seeing it set and then rise again a few hours later.

Bonfires were lit by our ancestors at various times of year, including Litha, to mark out the sacred days – the smoke can be used for purification and often cattle would be driven between two bonfires to symbolically purify them. St John's Wort, a popular herb used medically to treat many disorders, is traditionally picked at this time of year, with St John's Day being 24th June. Picking St John's Wort on midsummer's eve while skyclad is a common custom for female witches who are trying to conceive. The sun's power, the transition from the light, waxing half of the year to the dark, waning half, the golden colour of the corn growing tall in the fields, the pregnancy and vibrancy of the goddess – all these things combined make the summer solstice one of the most widely celebrated and one of the most public festivals. From Stonehenge to Callanish, people gather – pagan and non-pagans alike – to give their thanks and pay tribute to the power of sun.

The Oak King and Holly King engage in their eternal battle for the throne – at midsummer, the Oak King is slain by the Holly King but he returns in six months' time to regain the crown and rule the first half of the year.

Here is an adaptation of the Litha ceremony my coven held one year – kept deliberately short as we had a several young children present. Cast the sacred space as normal and have branches of oak and holly on the altar and a few ribbons – orange, gold and red to represent the sun.

Priestess:

It is the festival of Litha, the summer solstice, the height of warmth and bounty of the earth are celebrated in this rite. A time of being outdoors enjoying friendships and the first signs of the coming harvest as crops begin to grow, fed by the sunlight of the god. This is a time of feasting, watching the sun set and rise as we honour the god and goddess, bringers of love and happiness, warmth and comfort. At Litha, the god as Oak King is challenged to his place on the throne by his dark, winter-self, the Holly King.

(At this point the two kings circle and parade around each other).

As the Oak King is slain and the Holly King takes control, there is no mourning for all is as it should be and the cycle continues.

Oak King:

I give up my mantle (lays an oak branch on the ground) as is right and I pass over my power to my brother, my father, my other self, the Holly King.

Holly King:

I have bested you before and now I best you again, fairly and honestly I take power over you (throws his holly branch over the oak). I am the King! I am the returning Holly King!

Priestess & coveners cheer:

Long live the Holly King! Long live the Holly King!

Priestess:

Holly King, Holly King take your prize,
The Oak King surrenders to you with pride.
Goddess and God unite as one, Holly King, Corn Queen,
Hale to thee! Hale to the Goddess, hale to the God!

Ribbons are taken from the altar and tied to a large branch to represent wishes and desires and things we are grateful for. The Holly King parades around the circle, greeting all coveners and giving a little gift (a sweet or a flower) to the children. The circle is taken down and then the celebratory party or barbeque begins.

Fiery Passion

Beltane and Litha are probably the most passionate and lusty times of the year with the god and goddess at their most fertile and with the sun heading towards and reaching its peak, these two sabbats are associated with the element of fire. Try this spell to bring more fiery energy and passion into your life.

Use a red or orange candle as the focus and cast your circle, having already put everything you need on the altar which should preferably be decorated with a red cloth or a few rose petals scattered about – wear something red, have a pre-ritual bath, wear something sexy and spray on some perfume – if you are in a relationship you could do this spell with your partner and see how it spices up your evening! Think of a few key words that you associate with passion and love.

Hold a pin or the tip of your athame into the flame of a small altar candle and use the warm tip to inscribe your words into the red candle, saying them over and over out loud. *Love, passion, kissing, lusty, sexy.* Now use a drop or two of rose oil mixed with a carrier like almond or olive oil to anoint the red candle, rubbing the oil into the grooves of the words you carved.

Light the red candle as you say this chant, focusing all the time on your goal and then close your circle – or if you are working with your partner you might want to enact the great rite before closing.

Goddess of passion and love that's true; Aphrodite, Venus, I call to you.
Horned god, wild and free, Pan, Cernunnos, I call you to me.
Sunlight strong and golden warmth, kindle the passion of fire within;
Let my life from now on be filled with passion and power from deep within.
Ancient Ones, hear my call, let this spell work for the good of all!

Lammas/Lughnasadh

1st August – a fixed date. This is the first of the harvest festivals and is a time to give thanks for the first fruits of autumn and to all the things we have achieved or attained throughout the year so far. Lammas means 'loaf-mass' and it is the season when the first harvest of the year is ready – corn is a good representation of this and wheat-based products are put on the offering plate for the sabbat – cakes, pastries and biscuits and especially home-made bread.

Some witches call it Lammas, others Lughnasadh, which means a 'feast for Lugh', Lugh being the god/king of the Tuatha De Danann who learned the secrets of agriculture, sowing, ploughing and harvesting, from the Fomors in return for sparing their captured leader, Bres. Corn is tall in the fields and the Holly King starts to grow stronger and although the sun is still high and warm, the days are getting gradually shorter. We give thanks, not just for the food on our table, the flowers in our gardens and the material things we have, but we give thanks too for the intangible things like kinship, laughter, love and friendship and the many other things we have been blessed with.

Pagan camps and open rituals occur all over the country at Lammas and culminate in a ceremony where the god is given a token sacrifice to acknowledge and give thanks for all that we have been given. Things we have been literally given, things we had to buy, things we had to work damn hard for – the gods appreciate an attitude of gratitude and I know that sounds like a hippy cliché but it's also true. Giving something away as a token of thanks in offering to the Old Ones, the nature spirits, our ancestors, paves the way for more good things to come into our lives as well as honouring our gods. It doesn't have to be anything deep and meaningful or expensive – I know one gentleman witch who always carries a small leather pouch filled with herbs and roots to burn as an offering. Work your offering and sacrifice into the Lammas ritual and burn it on a fire or bury it in the ground or hang it up in a tree with thanks.

Lammas is associated with baking and bread-making in my house and I will never forget one year I had been helping out at an organic allotment collective for the day and was given free rein to forage for the blackcurrants which were just starting to look good and juicy. I gathered enough to make a big vat of jam and to pass the time while I waited for the scorching hot jam to cool for a few hours in the jars, I decided to team it up with some home-made bread that I pounded, raised and baked. The bread and jam were ready at the same time and that simple harvest was such a treat. Home-made produce is ideal for Lammas and your friends and neighbours will love you for it if you host a party or an open ritual and serve up something tasty that you made yourself.

A Lammas Loaf

1lb strong flour (white or wholemeal)
2tsp of dried yeast
1tbp olive oil
Warm water to mix
Pre-heat the oven to approx. 220C / 425F / Gas 6.

Mix the flour and yeast together and stir in the olive oil. Gradually add water – which should only feel warm not hot or it will kill the yeast – and mix to a stiff dough. Turn out onto a floured counter and begin to knead the dough. If it's too sticky, add a little more flour. As you knead the bread you can really put some effort into it, using your hands to stretch it back and forth, pulling it over itself and pushing it down again. To add a little extra magic, as you are kneading the dough, focus on love and joy and happy times ahead for all of those who will eat it. Carry on kneading for around five minutes or so and place in a clean, lightly covered bowl in a warm (not hot) place for approximately one hour. After this time, the bread should have risen to twice the original size. Turn it back out onto a floured surface and knead again for a few minutes. Shape into rolls or two small loaves and place on greased baking sheets. Cover loosely with a clean tea-towel and leave until doubled in size. Place in the centre of the oven for ten to fifteen minutes for rolls and around twenty to thirty minutes for larger loaves. The bread is ready when it sounds hollow if you knock on the bottom of it.

Mabon/Madron

20th - 22nd September, depending on astrological alignment, the druid festival of Alban Elfed, this is the autumnal equinox when days and nights are of equal length again. As Ostara looked forward to the brighter, longer days ahead, now Mabon is a time of preparation for the colder and longer nights of winter. Late September is always associated with harvest – more specifically, this is the end of the harvest season and themes for the Mabon ritual can revolve around giving thanks, completion and preparation.

As we see the long evenings of summer gradually become darker and colder, sending us indoors earlier and earlier, there are still some very warm and sultry days and of course, when we are outdoors in the autumn, we cannot help but notice the colours of the leaves and foliage all around us changing so dramatically. Those burnished amber, gold, red and orange leaves are the hallmark of autumn – bring in a handful of crisp, colourful leaves or berries or nuts to decorate the altar.

Mexican gods' eyes are pretty little crosses wound with colourful threads and hung in the house to repel evil spirits. They are very easy to make and an ideal Mabon craft for children and adults alike as an altar decoration in Mabon colours. Simply gather two sticks of about six inches or so in length and a selection of yellow, orange, gold and red threads, wools and ribbons. Hold the two sticks together to form a cross and tie together securely at the centre. Choose a bold colour for the centre and start to wind it around the cross, swapping colours as you feel like as you go round and round. It helps to hold the cross fairly flat so you can see the pattern taking shape and turn the cross round as you go. The thread passes over the top of the first stick, round the back and underneath it, back over the top of the same stick and then across to the next stick, wrap it around that one and then the next and so on, over and under and round and round. Make sure you loop the thread over the top of each stick in the same direction every time. Tie off when you reach the outside of the cross and leave a long enough end of yarn to hang it up with. I tend to use a blob of fabric glue or my glue-gun to make sure the knots don't come undone. Children can tie acorns from the bottom of the gods' eyes or feathers and brightly coloured leaves coated in a thin layer of clear glue to strengthen them.

The goddess of the harvest at Mabon is surrounded by animals, baskets of corn, apples and berries. She is budding with pregnancy and holds a sheaf of wheat in her hand. She is the Roman goddess, Ceres, or if you prefer, Greek Demeter. Corn dollies made out of plaited corn sheaves are still common and have a charm all of their own. Traditionally the last sheaves of corn to be harvested contains the spirit of the corn and in order to keep that spirit safe, the corn dolly made from it is hung up in the house over winter, thus ensuring that the spirit of the crop – so important to our ancestors who relied on these precious crops – would be kept alive and warm and be cherished and nurtured, ready to return to the fields when the sowing begins again in spring.

The goddess of Mabon is the mother goddess of the earth and all its bounty – all the efforts put in by our farmers over the year, the warmth of the sun, the nourishment of the earth – all of this comes to a head at Mabon and anyone who still grows their own produce will be busy reaping and preserving as much as possible to last over the winter. There's a high level of satisfaction in growing even a small amount of your own food over the year and picking fresh vegetables and herbs at Mabon. Even people like me (not in the least bit green-fingered, I can kill off a spider plant inside a month) can manage to successfully grow a decent crop of potatoes and pulling them from the ground in September, getting your hands dirty with the soil is a very good grounding exercise – with the added bonus of the freshest organic produce you could ever wish for.

The harvest of the season is not just seen as one of agriculture but a spiritual harvest – think back to Imbolc when you made a wish, a spell or a promise of something that you wanted to achieve. Did you really work hard to get it? Did it come to you easily? Did you give up or are you still working at it? Are you happy that you put in enough effort or did it really not seem worth it in the end? Whatever the results, you will have achieved something as a direct effect of making that pledge or casting that spell. Maybe you learned a valuable lesson if you realised that what you thought you wanted was not what you actually needed or perhaps you are revelling in the success of your endeavours. Things don't come along and just fall in our lap – if we have a fantastic life, it's because we made it so. Give thanks to the lessons you've been granted this year. Give thanks for the people who have made your life special.

Cleanse and Balance

Lammas and Mabon are the first signs we have of the year winding down towards winter but even so, the days are warm enough for a t-shirt and outdoor rituals. It's a time of balance when we are not quite done with summer but we are nevertheless preparing for winter. It's neither one thing nor the other, especially with the night and day balance of the equinox at Mabon and, moving around the circle of the elements, we come to water. Water represents our emotions – think of tears of joy and tears of pain, the waters of childbirth. This exercise is a gentle, unobtrusive type of healing magic that acts as a cleanser for the body and soul and it's virtually effortless so there's no reason not to give it a go. Take a small piece of moonstone and leave it outside or on a windowsill for a month to absorb all the power of each moon cycle and then place it in a glass of water or in your water filter overnight during a full moon. The following morning, remove the crystal and drink the water, feeling the essence of the moon and the balance of water, entering your body.

> *I drink this water as a cleansing tonic, to balance my emotions and harmonise my soul. I am renewed and cleansed; I am balanced and whole.*

Samhain

31st October, a fixed festival date, Samhain is pronounced sow-een (sow rhymes with cow). Samhain is the real beginning of winter and our farming forefathers had to slaughter any livestock that were weak or small – farmers know how many cattle they can realistically feed over winter and it makes sense to only feed the strongest and healthiest and sacrifice the rest to feed the family in the meantime and preserve that meat with salt to make it last. Similarly, with the limited medical care of medieval times and earlier, life for the sick and elderly in the house could be touch and go over winter and the Cailleach, the goddess of the dark and cold, was always ready and waiting to take the souls of the newly dead.

In Mexico Samhain is known as El Dia de los Muertos, meaning literally the Day of the Dead, the time when the ancestors are honoured. Brightly coloured skulls (sugar skulls) painted with flowers and glittering with gems are paraded through the streets in a three-day festival that starts on 31st October, when the spirits of children return to spend time with their families, and culminating in a huge feast and celebration on 2nd November when adult souls return for the party laid in their memory.

We also honour the dead at Samhain here in Britain but just as our Beloved Dead can visit us, so can evil spirits and demons. Pumpkins and turnips carved into a Halloween lantern originated in an old Irish legend. Jack was an Irish sinner who had tricked and trapped the devil. When the devil finally escaped he refused Jack entry into Hell, nor could the unfortunate soul gain entry to Heaven and as a result he wasforced to walk the earth evermore. The devil took pity on Jack and gave him a burning coal to light his path, Jack put the coal inside a hollowed turnip, hence the term 'jack-o-lantern'. Trick or treating, love it or hate, is a corruption of an older custom too. In order to appease the wandering spirits, householders would make 'soul cakes' or 'dumb cakes'. A silent baking session by the women and girls of the house ensured that when souls came knocking, there was plenty to offer them. There are numerous recipes for soul-cakes – hundreds of them, really – but any cake or bread will do if you prepare it in the traditional silence and offer it to the Beloved Dead.

Divination is popular at Samhain, often using food *(see also chapter ten)* such as apples and nuts. Two nuts in the hearth of a fire represents two lovers – if the nuts spit and fly apart as they heat up, the lovers' fate is likewise to spit and fly apart from each other; if the nuts jump and start towards each other, the couple have a favourable outlook. Apples for bobbing are carved with a young man's initials and unmarried girls pluck out the apples with their teeth to see if they are destined to fall in love with the bachelor they desire. Scrying with a dark mirror or in a black bowl filled with water is ideal for Samhain as the darkness of the scrying surface fits with the season.

There are almost countless customs and traditions of Samhain, interspersed with the likelihood of human sacrifice on the sacred bonfire as an offering to the dark gods of death and winter. Pumpkin and turnip lanterns to scare away demons; making mischief while disguised as a spirit or ghost; apple bobbing to determine your future spouse; bonfires, parties and divination. Entire books could be written on the subject of Samhain without ever reaching the end of folklore that wraps around it. For now, let's go back to the old winter hag, Queen of the Snow, she who lives in the cold mountains – the Cailleach. A goddess of death and winter, decay and endings, the Cailleach comes down to tear the last of the golden leaves from the trees to hasten the onset of winter. She reaps all that is no longer needed, taking it away to die so that it can be renewed and reborn. The Cailleach may bring death and endings but she isn't to be feared for without her gift of death there can be no rebirth.

Whether you choose a Hallowe'en party or Samhain ritual is down to personal choice and may depend on how public and open you are with your family and neighbours. Whatever the case, if you or your coveners have children, make sure you help them to carve out a few pumpkins and get them all stirring the big pot of soup that you make with the pumpkin's flesh. As the children – or adults – take turns to stir the soup, visualise that with every circle of the spoon, love and harmony is pouring into the dish for those who will eat it.

Have a go at divination with each person present picking an ogham stave, rune or angel card out of a bag. Put a big plate of sliced apples out for people to eat and another set of apples for apple bobbing.

Keep a place open at the Samhain feast for the Beloved Dead to return and join you, honour your loved ones with a photograph on the altar, remember them with stories and offer them soul-cakes.

At Samhain a fire is lit, even if only a candle indoors, and letters are written to the Cailleach in silence. Ask her to take away those things you no longer want – pain, jealousy, hatred, poverty, sadness, grief, bad habits, bitterness, anger. Without reading it, burn your paper and give it to the Cailleach in the ashes and smoke.

Yule

20th – 22nd December, another festival determined by the date of the actual winter solstice, Yule is the druid ritual of Alban Arthan. This marks the dead time of year, the shortest day and the longest night. Christmas has taken over from Yule as the dominant winter celebration although even the modern commercialism has undertones of the old beliefs. The Yule log is one aspect which is still nice to uphold, for example. On dark, winter nights a fire would be lit to keep away the cold and at Yule the fire was especially significant and reminiscent of the sun which was about to return to the world. A log from the embers of the Yule fire is kept back and is then used to light the fire in the hearth the following Yule. Pagans who are lucky enough to have an open fire or wood burner still do this today, keeping the Yule log safe throughout the year. The rest of us have to make-do with logs in the form of chocolate covered swiss-roll cakes – such a hardship!

I am often asked how I celebrate the Christmas season by newcomers to the Pagan path and by curious outsiders. I answer thus: I celebrate Yule on the solstice, it's my religious festival. Honouring and giving thanks for all that I've gained over the previous year, all the achievements I've reached, the friendships, holidays, good times and bad. I hold this Yule celebration with my pagan family (and sympathetic friends and family). I make at least two chocolate log cakes and have a big party with a feast or ritual and give out small gifts, normally hand-made, for my guests. One year I wrote a poem and printed it on scrolls tied up with ribbons for each guest to take away, another time, I made chocolate truffles and peppermint creams as a token gift. This gift-giving is a hang-over from my child-hood Christmas celebrations and I still enjoy it. The act of giving to others is always done with no expectations of anything in return but for continued good-will and friendship.

On December 25th, I also get together with family to share food and drink and the company of the people I love. The commercialism of the season is dreadful but I manage to avoid the worst of it by simply telling people I don't want gifts from them and if I decide to give them something, it's a token of my love for them and normally something hand-made – once I knitted hats for everyone, another year I made wine. So the 'big day' itself is wrapped up in memories of my childhood, spent with all my family and the closeness we share with each other and I love to be able to continue that family tradition. But I don't celebrate Christmas, I just have two days – 21st and 25th to celebrate Yule in my own way. One day is pagan-oriented, the other revolves around family and at both events, there is an over-riding theme of kinship, appreciation and love. One other thing I love to do is to walk out of doors with all the signs of deep winter around me. The bare trees and the rain-fall or snow, the wind and the chill and the darkness drawing in so quickly in the early evening. Warm layers of thermals stave off the worst of the cold but still it bites at our faces and nibbles our toes. Coming inside to warm up with a hot drink and a cosy home with cuddles on the sofa is made all the more special for all of that cold and frost outside.

Winter is harsh, the trees are bare, the ground is hard and cold and nothing is growing, nothing seems alive. Even in my own life, I notice that from Samhain to Imbolc there is little going on socially. It's a no-time, a transition time. Another good reason to celebrate Yule is to break the monotony of winter, lighten up our lives and have a good time, secure in the knowledge that now the year has reached its darkest point and the next day's dawn will be that tiny bit earlier and the whole day that little bit longer as the sun begins to climb back to its height once more.

The solstice may hide its secret well but it's there – the goddess finally sees the birth of her child, the child of light and promise in the new born sun king. The Holly King of midsummer is challenged and defeated by his brother-self, the Oak King. The sun is at its turning point, the first rays of morning light will break through the sky that fraction sooner in the morning and the seeds and bulbs buried deep in the earth are not really dead, only dormant, and that hard frost will force them into germination in just a few short weeks.

Yule activities include making decorations for the house, the tree and the altar. Two pieces of felt cut in the shape of a goddess figure, sewn with coloured thread and stuffed lightly, can be hung from the tree. Bunting or brightly coloured paper chains can be made by cutting up old magazines and has the added benefit of keeping young ones occupied for hours. Make a salt-dough and bake into pentacle shapes or bake and decorate a chocolate log and mince pies.

I am the Snow Queen of Winter, the hag, the crone, the Cailleach, goddess of death and decay. Make a gift for me of your troubles and woes, let me take your grief and fears away.

I am the Holly King, ruler of these last six months, pay homage to me for I am great and I am he who must be slain for the earth to be renewed.

I am the Oak King, challenger to the throne, I take the mantle of the new year and in my crowning I offer you the light of the new world. I am the Oak King, ready to be reborn.

I am the goddess who brings death and out of that death I give new life, the Oak King, the child of sunlight and promise, reborn. All hale him! Hale to the Oak King! Hale to the Oak King! Hale to the Oak King!

Earthy Visions

Samhain and Yule are the ending times of the year, the time of winding down and taking stock of what you've gained. The season of winter is aligned with the element of earth, with trees, caves, manifestation. Try this earthy visualisation.

Make sure you won't be interrupted, that you're warm enough and comfortable. No need to cast a circle, but you might want to put on some incense and use some deep relaxation techniques to get into a meditative state.

Now, clearly see yourself lying down on the ground, on the bare earth or on grass or a bed of heather. Somewhere natural, perhaps beneath the spread of an ancient yew or birch tree. Picture it with absolute clarity, so clearly that you can feel the earth beneath your skin as you sink down, eyes closed, darkness all around you. Feel yourself as one with the ground, a blade of grass tickles your fingertips and you can feel yourself starting to slowly sink, gently. The earth is shifting slightly beneath you. It makes space under you so that gradually, you are moving deeper into the ground, sinking slowly and as you sink, the earth piles up around you. The earth holds you safely and comfortably, wrapping soft roots around you, holding you snuggly and lovingly. The earth scatters all over you and you become completely buried by it, completely safe and comfortable. You can still breathe and you can still hear. The silence of the earth is broken by a whisper. The earth itself speaks to you … be still … listen.

The earth around you, the roots and shoots, begin to shift slightly, gradually releasing you, slowly the earth uncovers you and your body begins to rise as the ground scatters beneath you. As you rise up to the surface and lie once more on the ground, on the grass, remember the secret the earth spirit whispered to you. Feel yourself fully out of the ground and lying in warm sunshine. Gradually come back to where you are now. Take enough time to come back to the here and now slowly, no rush. Move your fingers and toes, stretch, slowly sit up and have something to eat and drink. Write down the secrets of the earth.

And so the Wheel of the Year turns again and we head towards Imbolc…

CHAPTER 3

Moon Magic and Celebrations

Witches have called on the power of the moon for centuries. Wiccans still use the energy of the moon for spell casting, ancient and modern poets wax lyrical about its brilliance and photographers capture its haunting beauty with stunning pictures from earth and space. As school children, we are taught that the moon does not shine itself – it only reflects the light of the sun, but apart from this, how much do we actually know about the moon?

The moon has three obvious phases, waxing, full and waning. It takes 29.5 days for the moon to complete a full cycle from new moon to new moon. The waning moon is seen as a 'C' shape and the waxing moon a reversed 'C'. The word gibbous, often used to describe the moon, applies only when it is seen as larger than a semi-circle but is not yet a full moon. The moon's day time temperature is a massive 243°F and it is approximately 238,000 miles away from us. We often talk about the effect the moon has on us here on Earth and it's true that the gravitational pull of the moon does have an effect on the oceans. Tides at a full and new moon are slightly higher than tides at the first or last quarter.

There is still some controversy about mankind's visits to the moon and many conspiracy theories give a whole range of explanations to, allegedly, prove that the moon landings were staged on *terra firma.* However, the lunar space missions have gone down in history as one of humankind's most significant achievements, so for now we will take them as fact instead of fiction. Neil Armstrong and Edwin 'Buzz' Aldrin landed the Eagle lunar module and carried out the first ever human moon-walk in July of 1969. There were a total of eight moon landings between 1969 and 1972, with astronauts bringing back samples of moon rock and leaving commemorative plaques on the surface. The last of the astronauts to walk on the moon was Eugene Cernan, at the end of the Apollo 17 mission. All this science may not seem to have much relevance to paganism and witchcraft, but bear with me because here's where it starts to get really interesting!

Moon Trees

In 1971 the Apollo 14 mission made its trip to the moon with a crew of three astronauts. One of the three was Stuart Roosa, who had a long history of working with trees as a smoke-jumper, putting out forest fires for the US Forest Service. Roosa, with his love of and connection to nature, took along around five hundred tree seeds collected by the US Forest Service for lunar orbit.

Roosa manned the command module Kitty Hawk and did not actually set foot on the moon itself but remained in its orbit while the lunar module Antares made the landing. Comprising of Loblolly Pine, Sweetgum, Douglas Fir, Redwood and Sycamore, the tree seeds were germinated on return to earth and many of the resulting trees are still doing very well. Although the seeds only went into lunar orbit and not strictly to the moon itself, the trees still became known as Moon Trees. So many people wanted to have a moon tree that cuttings were taken and the resulting trees were termed half-moon trees. There are at least 450 moon trees spread far and wide across the globe, mainly in America but also in Brazil, Switzerland and Japan. As a witch, I wonder what it would be like to hold a full moon Esbat ritual beneath the spreading branches of a tree that had its beginnings in orbit around our moon!

Once in a Blue Moon

Astronomical data detailing the moon's course through the skies and through the zodiac constellations is helpful for Pagans in pinpointing specific events such as a lunar eclipse – a time not only of astronomical interest but also a significantly powerful time for ritual magic. A total lunar eclipse is not as common as a total eclipse of the sun but they are seen by more of us more often. The path of totality of the solar eclipse is only visible in the sky from a narrow band of the earth. The moon's eclipse, however, is visible from half of the earth – wherever it happens to be night during the eclipse and unlike a solar eclipse, it is completely safe to view with the naked eye. A lunar eclipse is caused by the sun, the earth and moon lining up exactly so that the earth's shadow, or umbra, falls directly onto the moon. The moon is still visible during an eclipse due to the sunlight being refracted around our atmosphere and falling indirectly onto the moon. The atmosphere around the earth creates a filter, screening out blue light but red and orange light still passes through, giving the moon a dull reddish or orangey appearance or darker shades of red and orange, depending on earth's meteorological conditions at the time.

It's also the earth's atmosphere which provides us with the expression 'once in a blue moon,' despite the commonly held belief that a blue moon is the second full moon in a single month or the thirteenth full moon in a complete year. Throughout history there have been times when the moon actually *does* appear to be blue in colour. In September 1958 a massive forest fire in Canada sent dust and smoke into the earth's upper atmosphere and caused the appearance of a blue moon. The 1980 eruption of Mount St Helen's and the 1883 Krakatoa eruption sent massive plumes of ash and smoke high above the clouds. The debris and smoke can linger in the atmosphere between us and the moon, giving it a blue tinge when viewed from the earth. For as long as a whole month in the case of Krakatoa, the moon looked as if it were really coloured blue. There has even been a case a green moon sighting in Sweden in 1884, again the unusual colouring was caused by some kind of debris or dust released into the atmosphere.

Superstitions and Folklore

Science may explain the technical reasons behind things like a lunar eclipse or a blue moon, but the moon has captivated us beyond scientific curiosity and this is not restricted to those of a Pagan persuasion. It is reflected in the customs, superstitions, beliefs and folklore surrounding the moon.

It has long been believed that a full moon is a good time for divination and prophecy, especially if you happen to be a young woman looking for a suitor. One well known custom is that a young woman should gaze into a mirror at midnight on a full moon saying;

Moon, moon, tell unto me, when my true love shall I see?

Her lover will then appear behind her own reflection in the mirror. A variation of this is also done on Samhain eve for the same purpose.

The new moon is an omen of bad luck and misfortune if you first see it through glass yet if you see it out in the open from over your shoulder, the bad luck is reversed and good fortune is coming your way. To make sure that you will get good luck, you should bow to the new moon and then turn over a silver coin in your pocket or better still, take the coin out and show it to the moon. This old custom of turning over a silver coin in the light of the new moon is a form of attraction magic. As the moon begins to grow in size and brilliance, so the money in your purse will also grow.

Another piece of folklore says that a halo or haze around the moon is a portent of rain (a fairly reliable sign, as this haze is due to high moisture content in the atmosphere). Gardeners often consult an almanac in order to coincide their planting, sowing and harvesting with an advantageous moon phase.

Witches are said to gather in their covens at the full moon though the reality is that most witches will meet as and when the entire coven has the same night free in their busy diaries and believe me, this does not always coincide with the full moon!

If you have your hair cut during a waxing moon it will grow back more quickly than it will if you cut it when the moon is waning. The waxing moon is said to be a good time to become pregnant and the full moon a good time to give birth and makes for strong and healthy children.

It has long been believed that people and animals can act a little kookily around the time of the full moon. The word lunacy comes from the Latin Luna, which means moon. Several research studies have taken place to try and prove if there is a significant increase in outbursts of violence, psychosis and mental disturbance during a full moon and several of these have come up with very convincing data in favour of the theory. People who work in mental healthcare often do notice that significant numbers of patients are affected by the full moon. More people are admitted to psychiatric care at the full moon than any other time of the month. There have even been police reports confirming that general crime figures increase and there are more murders and petty crimes committed during a full moon than other times of the month.

The full moon is, of course, the night when werewolves change from human to wolf form. Although there have been documented cases of werewolves way back in the past, these can probably be put down to a case of wrongly diagnosed porphyria or lupus, rather than accounts of actual werewolves. Poor medical knowledge combined with fearful superstition of Shamanic journeys, often with the shaman dressed in animal skins, and inexplicable behaviour or unusual bouts of violence around the full moon would have made a convincing argument in favour of the existence of werewolves. Of course, we know today that werewolves are pure fiction – or are they? Supernatural creatures, like the Chupacabra, the mysterious mothmen, fairies and vampires are still reported today all over the world and as recently as 2011 there have been alleged werewolf sightings in the woods at Cannock Chase.

Another way the moon affects us is by its journey through the zodiac constellations. The moon travels through each of the twelve zodiac signs in just one month, spending two-and-a-half days in each sign before moving on, unlike the sun which visits each zodiac constellation for a month and completes the cycle in a year. Horoscopes deal with our star (sun) sign but we also have a moon sign which indicates the position of the moon in our zodiac chart at birth. There are plenty of websites offering a free service to work out where the moon appears at any given time, usually with predictions for the coming month, and any well-stocked library should have an ephemeris which you can use to work out your lunar sign. The moon's swift transition between the signs is magically beneficial; rather than waiting a whole month or several months for the sun to appear in a favourable zodiac sign to enhance our magic, we can time our rituals to coincide with the moon's influence in the constellations instead. It also means that our lunar birth sign is favoured for two days every month adding an extra spark of magical interest for anyone with an inclination towards astrology, especially if a full moon occurs when the moon is passing through our own star sign.

The moon is associated with menstruation and most women find that their menstrual cycle occurs at a particular time of the lunar month. Some Wiccan women have deliberately brought the two events into alignment to combine the magical influences of the full moon with the powerful time of the menses – one of the most powerful times for women in terms of performing spells and divination.

The full moon is the best time of the month for scrying with a witch mirror or in a clear pool of water with the moon reflected on its surface. Even better if the full moon coincides with the festivals of Beltane or Samhain, as the veils between the worlds are said to be at their thinnest at these times.

As an interesting aside to all this, on board the Apollo 14 with Stuart Roosa and Alan Shepard was Edgar Mitchell. While Roosa had his tree seeds and Alan Shepard took a golf club with him and played the first ever tee-off on the lunar surface, Mitchell took part in an experiment of an entirely different nature. He was interested in the field of telepathy and conducted a private experiment during the mission to see if people on earth could pick up telepathic messages which he transmitted from the moon. Due to minor delays and unforeseen factors, the experiment didn't appear to work too well as several earthlings reported that they were receiving the message on earth at a time when Mitchell was actually asleep on the moon. Perhaps it was the vast distances involved which slowed down the telepathic process? Mitchell retired from NASA in 1972 and went on to found the Institute of Noetic Sciences to encourage and conduct research into alternative healing, psychic abilities and the human potential.

Full Moon Names

There are normally twelve full moons in our calendar year and each one has a different name assigned to it. There are lots of variations on these names in Pagan circles, as many as twenty-five names for the same month in some cases, but here are the traditional English country names for the full moons.

January – Moon after Yule
February – Wolf Moon
March – Lenten Moon

April – Egg (or sometimes Paschal) Moon
May - Milk Moon
June – Flower Moon
July – Hay Moon
August – Grain Moon
September – Fruit Moon
October – Harvest Moon
November – Hunter's Moon
December – Moon before Yule

The Pagan names for the full moon are often allocated according to local custom or simply for the poetic sound of them which appeals somewhat more to the Pagan spirit. As there are so many names for the different moons, it's really a matter of personal preference. These are some of the most commonly used in witchy circles;

January – Wolf, Snow, Cold or Winter Moon
February – Storm, Snow or Death Moon
March – Chaste, Worm or Seed Moon
April – Seed, Awakening or Spring Moon
May – Hare, Flower or Planting Moon
June – Lover's moon or Summer Moon
July – Mead, Light or Blessing Moon
August – Wort, Plant or Herb Moon
September – Harvest, Hunter's or Wheat Moon
October – Blood, Death or Hunter's Moon
November – Snow, Tree, Oak or Divination Moon
December – Oak, Cold or Yule Moon

The Phases of the Moon

Witches of old honoured the moon and we continue to do so in our Esbat rituals. We use the power and influence of the moon in spells and rituals to bring good luck, healing and peace to those who need it. The moon's energy can be harnessed for enhancing psychic powers and bringing intuitive dreams. As the moon looks over us all, wherever we are in the world, we can all tap into its ancient power, whether we are witches or not. Once we understand which phase of the moon is in tune with our goals, we can start to build a ritual to help us manifest things in the physical world.

The moon is associated with dozens of goddesses around the world. Selene, Artemis, Diana, Arma, Arianrhod, Eithne, Coyolxauhqui, Arawa, Freyja and more have all been portrayed as a moon goddess and the moon as goddess has been revered by cultures across the globe from the Aztecs to the Celts. Witches associate the three moon phases with the triple goddess. She is the goddess of death, fertility, rebirth and creativity and appears in different guises throughout the lunar cycle.

The New Moon – The Maiden Goddess – young, beautiful and innocent, the Maiden Goddess is represented in the new and waxing moon. She represents our desires, our dreams, new love, creativity, inspiration, fertility, birth, purity and beginnings. As well as being pure, the Maiden Goddess is full of life, vitality, playfulness and allure. The new moon and waxing phase are a good time for magic concerning these things – new ventures, planting, inspiration, planning and dreams. Also under the influence of the Maiden Goddess and the new moon are healing, self-improvement, new projects, fertility, increase, job-hunting and new homes.

The Full Moon – The Mother Goddess – loving and nurturing with a heavily pregnant belly, the Mother Goddess is seen in the full moon. She represents maturity, friendship and family, enduring love, stability, growth, success, achievement, fulfilment, materialisation and completion. The full moon can be used for any kind of magic as the moon is at its most powerful at this time, but is especially useful for divination, protection, mothering, bringing things to fruition, transformation, gestation, materialisation of dreams and desires, success, increased wealth and the completion of projects.

The Waning Moon – The Dark Goddess or Crone – an aged and wise woman, knowledgeable, intuitive, the Crone is connected with the waning and dark moon. She offers protection from harm, release from suffering, death, decay, peace and endings. The Dark Goddess may reap our souls from the earth but she also sees us safely to the realms of the Otherworld so that we may be re-born and rise again. The dark and waning moon rule the darker side of life and in her Crone aspect, the goddess watches over the passing of souls. The Crone is the one we call on to help in rituals for banishing or binding, magic can be carried out for ending things, getting rid of bad habits, freeing yourself of unwanted ties or letting go of stress and banishing illness.

Blue Moon – the phrase 'once in a blue moon', as we have seen, is normally used to refer to the second full moon in a single month. Blue moons are powerful not because they are really a blue moon but because we have a second opportunity in one month to do spells for manifesting and achieving results.

The blue moon has great power and legend has it that whatever you wish for at this time is guaranteed to succeed. Magic for long-term goals or life-long ambitions will be successful so this is a good time to carry out magic for your deepest, most secret and heartfelt desires. As the blue moon is by its very description a full moon, it is ruled by the Mother aspect of the goddess.

Lunar Eclipse – even more powerful than a blue moon, a lunar eclipse can generate powerful magic and can be used for any type of positive magic which needs an extra boost. When you watch a lunar eclipse, it appears to be going through all three phases over a period of around two hours -

so you could time your ritual to incorporate every aspect of your magic – sowing the seeds of your wish, the creation and fulfilment of it and finally the end result and attainment of the wish.

Exact times and locations of a lunar eclipse are generally broadcast on the news in advance or in the wide range of Pagan media, Mind, Body and Spirit magazines and on astrology and astronomy related websites and media.

Moon Meditation

This moon meditation is a nice way to connect with the power and energy of the moon during any of its phases and especially during a full moon, when its influence on the earth is greatest. Use this ritual simply as a meditative state to gain peaceful energy and relaxation or for something more in-depth and serious if you wish. For a simple meditation like this, there is no real call for casting a formal circle unless you want to do it as part of a larger rite.

Stand or sit comfortably outside in a place where you can be undisturbed and safe, with the moonlight falling softly onto your face. Take several deep breaths and release any tension or worry. As you breathe out, let all your thoughts and concerns drift away from you; keep your mind still and calm. As you draw in the next breath, raise your arms high and visualise the moon energy coming down towards you. Breathe in the light of the moon and feel it filling you from head to toe, bringing the energy to rest deep inside your aura.

As you feel this energy coming down, let it start to collect and swirl gently in each of your chakras. Start with the root chakra at the base of your spine; let it gather for a short while around the chakra and then pull more moonlight energy into the sacral chakra, just below your navel. Again visualise the energy pouring into your hands and through your body to gather around the chakra. Next focus on the solar plexus chakra which is situated slightly higher than your navel, then your heart chakra, the throat chakra and third eye chakra, each time letting it fill your aura with the light of the moon goddess energy. Finally, bring the moonlight to concentrate in the crown chakra at the top of your head and see it as a white or silver light which builds up gradually to fill your aura completely.

Spend a few minutes simply feeling the moonlight embracing you … accept the power of the moon goddess energising you. If you are looking for guidance, ask questions either silently or aloud. Keep yourself open to any visions, images, thoughts or feelings that come into your mind as you do this.

Now give thanks to the triple goddess of the moon in your own words, either aloud or in your mind, and take your insights and energy with you as you return fully to the here and now.

Try this meditation at each phase of the moon's cycle to notice any subtle differences in how it affects you. Write this in your Book of Shadows or your journal if you have one.

Moon Magic

There are many ways of using the moon's influence in spells and rituals but here are a few things you can do that need little or no preparation and can be used for everyday magic to energise yourself and your life on a regular basis. Keep in mind the three major phases of the moon while carrying out these small magics and remember that any phase can be beneficial for any purpose with a little imagination in the way that you think about it. For example, if you think of the waxing moon as being suitable for healing but you happen to fall ill during a waning moon then you can work to get rid of the illness during the dark moon and as the moon becomes new and waxes again, you can focus on restoring your health.

Try this…

Leave a glass of water on your windowsill overnight with a piece of moonstone at the bottom. It will be energised by the moonlight and in the morning you can remove the moonstone and drink the water to fill yourself with positive moon energy. If you do this on the night before a full moon, you can use the water the following evening in your Esbat ritual. Keep the moonstone under your pillow to bring you sweet dreams and deep sleep.

Or this…

Crystals can be left on a window ledge to absorb moonlight; it will energize them and charge them with positive powers to be used for healing or spells. Try moonstone to open up your psychic centres, rose quartz for healing energy, amethyst to bring peace of mind or amber for happiness throughout the month. Wear the crystal around your neck or pop it under your pillow – you could even keep it in your purse so that you have it whenever you're out and about.

Spell casting…

To create a more elaborate moon magic spell, think of a positive goal you want to achieve. This might be a new job, peaceful resolution of conflict in the home, a new career, physical or emotional healing. After deciding which moon phase will work best with your intention, plan ahead to have some sacred time for a ritual to coincide with that moon phase. To maximise the potency of any spell you can combine this with appropriately coloured candles, crystals, relevant days of the week and so on. The table of correspondences *(see appendix)* is just the tip of the iceberg and your own intuition and research are necessary to build up a list of your own, more personally meaningful, correspondences. Coloured, anointed candles, herbs, crystals, runes, zodiac symbols, sigils and incense can all be used and charged to add to the success and strength of the spell.

I'll say it again - as with all of the spells and rituals offered in this book, this one can be used exactly as it is for those who are just starting out or can be adapted and changed if you have more experience and knowledge. It might seem odd to take a spell straight out of a book and change it to incorporate your own ideas, but the best spells truly are those we have developed ourselves. Above all, let common sense and intuition be your guide in coming up with spells that will work for you within the guidelines of the Wiccan rede.

Gather together a white or silver candle, incense, plain paper and pen, a glass of water and anything else that you will need in the circle such as incense, a wand or athame. Make sure you feel comfortable and relaxed before you start – spend a few minutes in peaceful contemplation of your intended result.

Cast the circle and light the incense and take it round the room, declaring that your space is made sacred and serene, a special place between the worlds for magic and harmony. See the boundary of your space as a circle of silver light which will remain in place throughout the rite. Return the incense to the altar and go to the four quarters of the circle invoking each element in turn, the Horned God and finally the Moon Goddess.

I call upon you, Triple Goddess of the Moon to be here within my circle and I ask you to give me your wisdom, your joyfulness and nurturing.

Use the tip of a pen or a pin to carve a word summing up your wish into the candle and focus on it as you light the candle saying:

As the candle burns and the moon turns,
So my desire is now set free, the Moon Goddess brings it to me,
Moon Goddess, hear my call, let this spell work for the good of all.

Place your glass of water in front of the candle so the flame is reflected in the water and say:

Goddess of the Moon, Gracious one,
I ask that you grant my wish,
Come into the water, come, come.
Let your magic be within my grasp.
Empower this water with your magic,
Let your power flow and grow, give to me my desire.
May this spell work for the good of all,
As I do will, so mote it be.

Focus again on your desire, visualise it clearly, see it coming to pass in your life and sit quietly in contemplation for a few minutes as you watch the flame. See the goal you want radiating out with the heat of the candle and see the moon energy bringing it back to you. Make a note of any thoughts that flow through you - at quiet times like this we can often receive insights to our problems and solutions we hadn't thought of can come to us in a flash of intuition.

Drink the water and silently give thanks to the moon goddess for granting your desire. Keep the candle burning for as long as you can, preferably until it has burned down completely. If this is not possible, relight it whenever you can over the next few days, focusing on the intention of the spell as you light the candle.

Once you have finished, give thanks to the moon goddess and close the circle as normal, releasing your sacred space by walking around it and let the silver energy dissolve harmlessly back into the ether with the candle's light.

Over the course of the next few weeks, you should carry out any actions in the real world which will help your situation – apply for jobs, be more tolerant towards family members, try new remedies for health and well-being or whatever else will aid you. Believe in the power of the moon and you will soon have your wish granted! It is said that we will receive our wish within one full turn of the moon's cycle so watch the sky and wait, secure in the knowledge that your wish is speeding along to you.

The Esbat

An Esbat is a celebration or working ritual in honour of the moon, usually carried out at a full moon, although you can also hold a moon ritual at any time of the month to honour each phase if it seems appropriate to whatever magic or healing work you're doing. Fertility magic, for example, is best saved for a new moon while banishing spells to get rid of something can be done at the waning or dark moon. The ritual structure of the Esbat remains the same as it is for any other ritual or Sabbat. Remember that everything given here is just a starting point and the more of your own ideas you include, the greater the benefits. Witchcraft isn't set in stone and you can add in or take away whatever appeals to you and feels right.

Full moon meetings are a useful time to carry out any training in a coven, to practice skills and try out spells, to come up with ideas and plans for any major Sabbats that are coming up. The Esbat also provides a suitable occasion for initiations if you are a long way from Imbolc; having said that, waiting those few extra months for the traditional Imbolc initiation gives the initiate the benefit of additional time to experience the practical applications of any teaching already given and to be more thoroughly prepared for the initiation itself.

Typically a full moon rite includes songs, poetry, dancing and drumming in honour of the moon goddess; you could also carry out a journey to the sound of drums or rattles to meet with your power animals or to speak with the goddess and god. It's a good time for divination, meditation or cleansing. Use the ritual to carry out any blessing and consecration of magical tools or to cleanse any crystals and candles for future spell castings. Charge amulets and talismans on the altar while you do the ritual or channel energy into a poppet for healing magic.

- Cleanse your working space and the auras of all participants.
- Cast the circle and invoke the elements.
- Invoke the goddess and god.
- Carry out consecrations and blessings of magical tools and jewellery.
- Any other work and teaching – spell casting, healing, divination etc.
- Raising energy with a cone of power for any magic worked.
- Poetry, dancing, songs or incantations in honour of the moon goddess.
- Ritual blessings of cakes and wine.
- Giving thanks to the goddess and god and the elements.
- Close the circle.

CHAPTER 4

Sun Magic and Celebrations

Wicca has a tendency to place a large emphasis on the cycles of the moon and its use and power in magic and rituals and with the moon being so closely linked to the cycle of the goddess who is venerated, sometimes more so than the god, it's easy to see why. Additionally, the moon runs its entire cycle in just one month so you never have to wait long for an appropriate phase for banishing magic or a new moon for a healing spell. While it would be folly to ignore the effects the moon has over us and to turn away from its usefulness in spell castings, it is by no means the only planetary body which can be harnessed in this way and although it does have a lot of significance, beauty and mysticism about it which is very appealing and romantic for the pagan soul, the sun also has a certain attraction which is hard to ignore. To do justice to the sun as we have with the moon in the previous chapter seems only fair – it is, after all, the most amazing creation – it gives us not only light but divides our time into day and night, provides us with regular seasons, enables all the flora and fauna on our planet to thrive and sustains us with the energy that makes all life possible.

Druid rituals for the winter and summer solstice are big events, honouring the sun and its birth, death and rebirth. From Stonehenge to the pyramids in Egypt and Mexico, huge structures have been erected all over the world that line up with careful precision to the first rays of light on the winter and summer solstice. Honouring the sun and its turning points has been part of our culture for thousands of years with sacrifice, perhaps human, certainly animal, to ensure the sun would rise again.

The Science Bit

Just one of over one hundred thousand million stars in our galaxy alone, our sun is a yellow dwarf star. It is 93,000,000 miles away from earth and 26,000 light years from the centre of the galaxy. In June, the Earth reaches the aphelion of its orbit and is further away from the sun by 1.5 million miles. Despite the vast distance involved, it takes only 8.6 minutes for the sun's light to reach earth.

Our sun is around 5,000 million years old, The sun is 1,300,000 times the size of the earth, give or take a few, and has a rotational period of 25.4 days at the solar equator. There are five layers to the sun, with the internal areas called, rather unimaginatively, the stellar interior and right at the centre lays the core layer where energy is generated and released in the form of gamma rays which are an energetic type of light.

To say the sun is hot would be nothing short of a dramatic understatement – the temperature at the surface, called the photosphere, is at least 5,500 degrees centigrade and the core temperature is a staggering fifteen million degrees. We tend to think that the sun is burning but if it had any solid mass it would already have burnt out completely. It is a globe of incandescent gas with nuclear reactions firing off in the core. Hydrogen, the most common element in the universe, acts as fuel for the nuclear fusion process which is on-going in the sun's core. The nuclei of hydrogen atoms combine within the core to make up the heavier element of helium with a ratio of 4:1. With each new helium atom formed, the sun loses a slight amount of mass and in the time it took you to read this far through the book, the sun is considerably lighter than it was when you started – but this won't add up to a significant loss for another five thousand million years or so, at which point the sun will turn into a red giant star with an intensified heat at the core and cooler outer layers. Following the red giant stage is a cooling period known as the white dwarf stage and finally, upon the sun's demise, it will be a black dwarf with seven dead planets still circling it. If all this sounds a little worrying, bear in mind the enormous time scale – the universe is still young in cosmic terms and it may not even be old enough for any black dwarf stars to have been formed yet.

The projected image of the sun (see below on eye safety) appears as a bright yellow sphere. Any smaller dark patches on this image are sunspots. Sunspots appear as dark spots because they are lower in temperature than the surrounding area by around two-thousand degrees. A sunspot is seen as a black-looking central umbra surrounded by a lighter area, the penumbra. Sunspots are usually seen in small clusters, though single spots are also common. The life span of a sunspot can be anything from just a few hours to a few weeks. Observing sunspots over several consecutive days shows the spot appear to move from one side of the sun to the other, this is caused by the sun's rotation and if it is especially large, it will be seen again on the other side as the sun continues to rotate. Sunspots are a type of magnetic phenomena, occurring where the magnetic force of the sun breaks through the photosphere and causes localised cooling.

Eclipses and partial eclipses of the sun occur when the moon passes fully or partially between the earth and the sun and only ever occurs when the moon is new and the sun and moon are in conjunction as seen from the earth. A total solar eclipse would be seen every month if the moon were perfectly circular, a little closer to the earth and on the same orbital plane, however the moon has an elliptical orbit so its path takes it far enough away that its apparent size is not big enough to totally block the sun. There are at least two and sometimes five, solar eclipses each year but a total eclipse is rare and the path of totally extremely narrow, making our chances of seeing a full solar eclipse quite rare. Eclipse parties are common with eclipse chasers or 'umbraphiles' travelling all over the world to see a total eclipse and celebrate the phenomenon with massive parties and raves.

★ While we can use binoculars and telescopes to view satellites, far off stars, moons and planets in our galaxy, **it is not safe to look directly at the sun in any way. Using a telescope or binoculars to look at the sun will cause permanent eye damage.** Even looking directly at the sun with the naked eye can cause eye trauma and damage. It is absolutely essential to use the correct equipment and image projection techniques if you want to observe the sun and an astronomy club would be the ideal place to get sensible and accurate information on how to do this.

The Folklore and Mythology

Associated with the god, rather the goddess, the sun is thought of as predominantly male. The sun has also been a major player in various creation myths. The Egyptian god of the sun was Atun or Ra, later known as Amun-Ra, the creating eye of the sun. The sun was the creative force rising out of primeval spirit or space and bringing all things into being. At the beginning of creation, Ra lay with his eyes closed in a lotus bud deep in the primordial waters and when he emerged, opening his eyes and revealing himself, he gave form to the air god Shu and the rain goddess Tefnut. In turn, Tefnut bore the earth god Geb and the sky goddess Nut who then went on to produce more gods – Nephthys, Set, Isis and Osiris. All living creatures, including the first humans, are said to come from Ra's tears and he created and ruled the first universe until a dispute with Isis, after which Ra withdrew back into the sky to sail his boat every night through the underworld until he emerged and rose again in the east. The image of the sun travelling on a giant sky-boat is seen in other cultures too –

the Norse goddess Sol or Sunni, is described as sister to the moon and is one of the very few female deities associated with the sun. Sol has a great sun-chariot that she rides in as she is chased across the sky by wolves. The solar deity of Hinduism, Surya, also travels in a chariot, this time pulled by seven horses, or sometimes a seven-headed horse – so bright was his light that his wife, Suranya, could not stand it and left him until he agreed to give up one of his eight bright rays. Surya is still worshipped in some Hindu temples at dawn.

The Celtic gods Lugh and Belenos are both associated with the sun. Belenos or Bel, means 'shining one' and the fire festival of Beltane, with its traditional 'bel' bonfires may take its name from Belenos. Lugh, as we have already seen, was worshipped across Britain as a sun god who gives his strength and energy to ensure the fertility of the land and he is portrayed with flames or rays of sunlight radiating out from him.

The Chinese believed there were ten suns which appeared in rotation on each of the ten Chinese calendar days. The Suns lived in the Valley of Light where Xi He, their mother goddess, would wash them and lay them to bed in the branches of a tree. The next morning a different sun would take its turn to shine down upon the earth – until, that is, they became bored with the routine and all ten of them appeared at once and spread themselves out all over the earth, making it incredibly hot. The Suns would not behave or go back to their usual routine no matter how much Xi He pleaded with them so an archer shot nine of them, leaving us with a single sun who now behaves himself quite well.

The Christian creation story starts almost immediately with the creation of the sun. "In the beginning god created the heavens and the earth. The earth was without form and void, and the darkness was upon the face of the deep. And god said *'Let there be light' and there was light.'*

Back on earth, we have numerous customs and sayings about the sun and sunsets. The old rhyme *red sky at night gives shepherd delight, red sky in the morning gives shepherds warning* is still well known even among townies and it has some basis in truth for meteorological reasons – if the air is clear of moisture as the sun sets in the west, this is reflected in the clouds to the east as a reddish-pink hue and indicates any rain has already come and gone. In the morning, a red sun rise means there is rain on the way for now the light of the sun shows up moisture in the clouds to the west and as Britain has predominately westerly winds, that rain is still on its way to us but if that rain comes early in the morning take comfort in the following rhyme: *rain at sevens means fine by eleven.*

Bright sunshine on your wedding day foretells a long and happy marriage and if your children are born at sun rise it will make them happy and wise while misfortune and dull-wittedness is saved for those born at sun set. Sunday, associated with the sun astrologically, is a propitious day to born on but is an unlucky day to change bed sheets, have your hair or nails cut or to sing a false note in church. Sunday is also a bad day to sign legal paperwork or to swear an oath.

Eclipses have a host of supernatural tales associated with them and have often been regarded as an omen of bad luck. Birds and insects behave as though night is falling, tweeting and roosting as the sun appears to set and then starting up again at the apparent sun rise a just a few hours later. The silence of the birds during an eclipse is truly eerie. Pregnant women of my grandmother's generation and earlier were supposed to wear a red girdle to protect their unborn child from the bad influences of an eclipse or their baby would be born with a cleft palate.

If the sun falls in such a way that your shadow is seen without its head on the winter solstice, it is said that great misfortune or death will come your way inside a year. It's not only our own sun but other stars that have folklore attached to them as seen in this little rhyme that is still in use: *Star light, star bright, first star I see tonight, I wish I may, I wish I might, have the wish I wish tonight!*

It has to be first star that you see and you must then wait until you see a second star otherwise you will not get your wish.

Shooting stars are not really stars at all but meteoroids passing across the earth's upper atmosphere but they are still supposed to be lucky if you see one. The best chances of seeing a falling star are advertised in the media and there are several large meteor showers every year, such as the Perseids and Leonids. It is often said the souls of the dead rise to live in the skies as a new star or even that every star we see is the soul of a dragon. These superstitions of souls living among the stars are very old and associated with the concept of the heavens being the dwelling place of the old gods.

The Solar Cycle

The solar year has two distinct phases, the waxing period runs from mid-winter solstice to mid-summer solstice and the waning phase from mid-summer to mid-winter. The waxing half of the year, ruled by the Oak King, is a period of birth or re-birth, youth and growth, a period of learning, playfulness and fertility. The waning half of the year is ruled by the Holly King and is a time of winding down, making use of wisdom and knowledge, maturation, reaping and harvesting and finally winding down to old age and death. We see the cycle repeated throughout the course of a single day too as the sun rises, reaches its peak in the sky, sets and finally disappears completely to return anew at dawn the following day. The sun god, as the rutting stag, the joyful hunter, is young and fairly rampant as we have seen, sowing his wild oats and having a jolly old lusty time – still he is a god of protection and provides for the future with the seeds and fertility of the land as well as the fertility of animals. When the darker half of the solar year comes along, we see the god as an elder, a wise man who uses his experience to guide others as a mentor and he has been seen in many stories as the ruler of the realms of the dead, the Lord of the Underworld, as in the story of Persephone and Hades.

Hades abducts Persephone, beautiful daughter of Zeus and Demeter, the corn goddess, and whisks her off to the underworld to be his consort but Demeter is so aggrieved by his actions that she brings a curse of winter to the earth, leaving it barren and lifeless. Zeus intervenes, calling for a compromise – Persephone can return to Demeter but must spend at least part of the year with Hades in the underworld, giving rise the season of deep winter while Demeter mourns her daughter until her return to the earth in spring. Persephone is treated very well by Hades, however, she is not a prisoner, rather he makes her the Queen of the Underworld.

This splitting up of the year into light and dark is a recurring theme in many legends and while the darkness, death and decay of winter seem negative, in truth, without that aspect of the god and nature, we would not be able to welcome and appreciate the return of the light, the abundance, fertility and life that the waxing sun brings us. The theme of sacrifice, of giving up one thing in order to gain something else, as Demeter sacrifices Persephone for a period of time, as the Oak King and Holly King sacrifice themselves to allow the power to change hands, can be a powerful theme for a ritual around either solstice.

Solar Meditation

Use a deep relaxation technique like the rainbow countdown *(see chapter five)* to get yourself into the journey state and have a go at this path working. Remember that although you don't always have to set up a formal circle for things like this, you should at least make sure you're grounded and maybe do some aura work beforehand and switch off your mobile phone. If you're not used to this type of journey work, you can always skip this part for now and come to back it at another time.

Sit or lie comfortably and do your relaxation so that you slip easily into the realms of the otherworld. Visit your place of power, your inner temple or sacred place, take plenty of time to really feel yourself there, to be fully present and aware of your surroundings in the realm of your sacred space.

It is night time and in the darkness you make out a winding path that you follow. This path leads you to the edge of a wide open space where a standing stone circle has been stood for thousands of years. Take note of how tall the stones are, how many, how wide, how large the circle. Enter the ring of stones and stand in the centre of the circle, turning to face each of the stones in turn. As you stand in the centre, taking in the age and presence of the standing stones, the sky begins to grow lighter. Sit facing the direction of the rising sun, sit in silence, in solitude.

As the sky becomes lighter and lighter, close your eyes and let those first rays of the morning sun come through the stone circle to bathe you in its light. Feel the subtle warmth of the sun on your skin, hear the calling of the birds as they greet the dawn. This is the first half of the year, the domain of the new born Oak King. It's the time of birthing, beginnings, associated with the element of air. Drink in the air that is tinged with the light of the new sun. As it rises, the sun starts to reach its full power and strength, the heat of noon touches your brow, the Oak King has reached the peak of his reign. This is the time of fire and passion, the height of the summer and the mid-point of the day. Now the sun slowly begins to set, very slowly, entering the waning time of the Holly King. At dusk the element of water is bringing things to you on its buoyant tides and you are bathed in a shadowy light that ebbs and flows and slowly weakens. Now the sun is setting, disappearing from view behind you and when the darkness descends towards midnight, the Holly King and the element of earth are at their height, earth brings materialisation and endings and so rebirth. As the darkness turns towards light again, with the birth of the sunrise in the sky once more and the Oak King taking the crown again, dawn brings with it a vibrant ray of sunlight that touches you.

As you sit and watch the cycle of the sun, think of how each aspect of it – waxing and waning, ebbing and flowing – relates to your path through life. What stage of the cycle are you in? What phase of the sun would benefit you most right now? Do you need the light and vitality of the summer solstice to shine down and give you strength or do you need the absence of the sun, the dying and rebirth of the Holly King at winter solstice so that you can let go of something and move forward with new ideas and a fresh outlook?

When you feel ready, give thanks to both aspects of the sun god and make your way back to the inner temple or sacred space you started from. Gradually begin to feel yourself in the place where you are now, feel your fingers and toes, breathe, open your eyes. In your own time, wake up to the here and now and write down your experiences and thoughts on the solar cycle in your book of shadows.

Solar Magic

This cycle of the sun brings all the elements into play in the course of just twenty-four hours unlike the moon which takes a full month to complete its cycle. No Book of Shadows would be complete without a section set aside for spells connected to the sun. While not as popular or well-known as moon magic, solar spells can prove more adaptable as they can be done at any time of the day, month or year; Of course, this twenty-four hour period is not a full solar cycle, but it does have an obvious effect on our planet – just listen to the birds at dawn and dusk if you are in any doubt of that.

Try this … to start off with here's a little saying that is a simple magic for the increase of wealth. Hold up a piece of gold at midday on the summer solstice and show it to the sun (mind your eyes), turn it in your hands so that it catches the sun and say this little chant three times.

Money Lords of the strongest sun, double my fortune and double my luck, Money Lords of the strongest sun, bring more money to me, to me, bring good fortune to me, to me!

Another simple way of using solar magic is to have a candle or small fire to represent the sun in your home or garden or a camp – often pagan camps and festivals will build a wicker man at the summer solstice, sacrificing it with fire as a way of saying farewell to the light half of the solar year and welcoming the waning half. Offerings or little sacrifices are placed inside the wicker man so that as it burns, our wishes, desires, bad habits etc are burned with it and released. Bonfires are a good way of making a symbolic sacrifice at Yule, or an actual sacrifice – giving up to the flames things that remind you of hard times, say a photograph of you looking happy with someone who hurt you for example.

Solar Spell for Happiness

During the first half of the year when it's found all over the countryside growing wild, gather a small bunch of heather at noon on a sunny day. Heather has been considered a lucky plant for generations, sold by gypsies in small bunches wrapped in foil and often given to brides on their wedding day for a happy marriage. Heather is Ur of the Ogham alphabet which again is a happy and fortunate sign of good luck, health, general happiness and a good omen all round. Now that you have your heather, put it in on your altar with red, orange or gold candles and for the best results, carry out this spell in the morning when the sun is rising, the phase of increase and prosperity. You could combine this with the influence of a new moon phase if you wanted to but as this is solar magic, make sure you still carry out this spell in the morning once sun has started to rise.

Place lots of solar symbols on your altar, a red cloth, gold coins or jewellery, something gold or orange that you can bury (even if it's a scrap of ribbon or paper) and of course, your sprig of lucky heather and an orange candle. You will also need a piece of wood or a small stone onto which you can draw the symbol of Ur, a long straight line with three smaller lines crossing it horizontally near the top. You could even just paint or draw the symbol onto a thick piece of card. For preference, you should do this spell outside in the light of the rising sun.

Cast a circle with invocations to the elements, welcoming in the goddess and god. Bless and consecrate the heather, candle, stone/card and the offering object at your altar and then light the candle as an offering to the sun.

As the sun starts to rise in the east, I light this candle as a beacon for prosperity and growth, for increase and good luck.

Pick up the heather sprig and hold it up the sun.

I charge this heather with the light of the sun, to bring me good luck and happiness.

Place it on your altar next to the candle and then draw the Ur symbol on your stone/card.

I bless this token with the element of air, fire, water, earth and spirit and I name it Ur, a symbol of good luck and happiness. Let this token be filled with the light of the sun.

Hold it to the sun and set it next to the heather and the orange candle and pick up your offering. Show it to the sun.

Rising sunlight, I give this (object) of mine to you in exchange for what I ask: joy, happiness, good luck and prosperity. Let all good things come into my life.

If possible, bury the object now, if not then keep it on the altar until you can do so.

As the sunlight grows, so shall my health, my wealth and my happiness increase. Power of the sun god, I ask of you, lend your powers to seal this spell. Let this work for the good of all, I as I do will, so mote it be!

Give thanks as normal and close your circle and keep the Ur symbol in your wallet, purse or hand-bag and hang the lucky heather up in your house where you will see it every day and preferably in a south-facing window where sunlight can shine on it. Let the candle burn all the way down or if you cannot then light it again first thing in the morning, focusing as you do on thoughts of increase, good fortune and general happiness.

Banishing & Binding Spells

If you are doing binding magic, rather than waiting for the dark or waning moon, you can tie your spells into the waning energy of the sun at sunset. Similarly, the sun's energy can be harnessed for new beginnings, creativity and inspiration at dawn and manifestation of desires and achieving goals at high noon. Midnight is not called the witching hour for nothing! The moon is high in the sky and the sun has long since disappeared over the horizon so why not use an appropriate moon phase together with absence of the sun?

Hey, You! Back Off!

I call this a back-off amulet because that's exactly the effect it has on people so if you have a particular person in mind who is bothering you, for whatever reason you just want them to back off and leave you alone, make a back-off amulet to ward them away. You will need two small thin sticks roughly two and a half to three inches long, black wool or thin black ribbon and red wool or ribbon in addition to elemental symbols on the altar and a photo if possible of the person in question and some thin black sewing cotton.

Carry out all your normal preparations for spell workings and collect everything you need so that you don't need to break either the circle or your concentration. It must be midnight as you make this amulet to get the full effect of the waning/dying sun and if you can, combine this with waning/dark moon too so that you have a double-whammy effect.

First do some grounding work and cleanse yourself thoroughly with smudging incense to get rid of any feelings of hatred or anger that may be associated with the person you're doing this for. If you need to, and this will depend on your reasons for wanting this person to back off in the first place, you might want to consider doing some emotional healing work first to rid yourself of bad feelings. Do not skip this part even if you only do a thorough grounding and aura cleansing, it's really important that you do this spell with peaceful intentions and no vehemence or bitter thoughts at all – you do not want this spell to reverse or place upon you any curse!

Now sit in silence and look for a moment at the photograph (if you you don't have one, write their name in bold letters on a piece of paper) focus on them clearly. In calm tones and without using words of blame, tell that person why you want them to leave you alone. Light a candle and take up the black cotton, pull off a long piece and hold it in the candle's flame until it breaks apart and repeat several times, breaking the thread in the flame at least nine times:

> *I break the ties that link us together, I break the connection between us, this link is broken. I sever this link, I sever this connection, the link between us now is broken.*

Burn the photograph in the candle flame and mentally see that person disappearing from your life, not harmed in any way, but irrelevant to your life and out of your way.

> *I discard you from my life, I banish you from my affairs, I cast you away and see you no more.*

Bind the two sticks with the black yarn and make a tiny Mexican eye, keeping the wool tightly bound and all the time willing that person to just leave you alone. Finish the amulet off by binding it with an outside edge of red wool and tie it off. Adapt the words below to suit your circumstances.

> *You are bound from doing me harm, you are bound from speaking to me, you are bound from coming near me. You are bound now to leave me alone. I speak to you (name the person) and I command you to BACK OFF! Ancients, Old Ones, hear my call, this charm will work for the good of all, as I do will so mote it be!*

Spend a good ten minutes or so visualising clearly that every time you see this person in future they are walking away from you. Consecrate the back-off amulet with the elements on your altar and close your circle down. When you can, go outside and bury the ashes of the photograph.

The amulet should be carried with you in a concealed place at all times and places where you are likely to see this person. If you do happen to see them, reach into your pocket, touch the amulet and clearly visualise them walking away.

Sunshine Protection

Here's a protective charm empowered by the sun. Carry this out at noon on a Sunday and if it's actually a sunny day, so much the better. Find a small gold coin or a piece of amber or similar sun-coloured token that you can use. Find some orange or red material and make it into small pouch – if your sewing skills are not up to the task, you can find small cloth bags like the ones used for wedding favours in a craft shop, usually for less than twenty pence, which you could use instead. Have orange or bright yellow candles on the altar along with a pinch of saffron if you can get it or a small piece of root ginger, a small pentagram, a ring and a spiny or thorny flower like a thistle or rose.

Prepare your sacred space in the sunshine and sit and meditate for a while, letting the goodness of the sun soak into your bones and onto the altar. Feel yourself free of worries, completely safe and entirely comfortable as you bask in the sun. Feel that golden light all over you, creating a bubble around you, inside of which all is positive and healthy. Now turn to the altar and consecrate the items, including the pouch.

Give a little prayer to the sun, something like this:

> *Sun god of the waxing year, I offer you this simple prayer, bestow upon me your protection and keep me safe from harm. Let your power be held within this charm, as I do will, so mote it be.*

Light the candles and put the pentagram, petals from a thorny flower, a fiery spice, the ring and gold coin and/or amber into the pouch and close the bag tightly. Hold it up to the sun and as you do, feel that protective golden light radiating down again, all around you.

> *Great shining god of the waxing sun, I call on your power, give me protection in this charm each and every hour. Ancients, Old Ones, hear my call, let this spell work for the good of all.*

Bask in it and visualise it clearly – all that protective energy now conferred to the charm bag in your hand. Leave it on your altar in strong sunlight for as long as possible and thereafter keep it in your car for safe travel, hang it up in your home as a protection from unwanted visitors or keep it with you as you go about your regular day.

CHAPTER 5

The Power of the Witch

Being a witch is not about fancy robes and leaving your witchy books on display on the coffee table to make a statement when you're expecting visitors – it's about being a witch on the inside. This means different things to each of us, of course, but I hope that more witches would agree than disagree with me when I say that being a witch is in the everyday things we do. Welcoming the ancestors into our homes, talking to our plants, caring for others, connecting to our natural environment. Being a witch every day means stirring that pot of stew with loving intentions towards those who will eat it, hanging rosemary in the house for good luck, keeping smoke quartz by our computers, taking care with our words so that we don't knowingly hurt people's feelings, bringing mistletoe into the house for Yule, saying hello to magpies, turning over a new leaf when we see it fall and feeling our connection to the mother goddess when we step out barefooted into the garden to bring the washing in. Being a witch is about so much more than spells and magic. It's about celebrating the different seasons of the earth and the cycles of life we all go through. It's listening to the sounds of nature, feeling empathy for other living creatures, using healing herbs or crystals or reiki to help others, offering a shoulder to cry on if your divination client is full of grief. It's a journey that has no end (and often no clear beginning either, come that) but that leads us to different places, different experiences and different people as we learn, grow and develop.

Some of us have fantastic psychic skills with the ogham, runes, tarot or a crystal ball, some of us are kitchen witches, always brewing or stewing something healthy, tasty and filled with love, some of us are excellent at healing; one witch friend of mine is a medical herbalist and another woman in my social circle is a sports masseuse who adds a dash of reiki and energy to her therapy sessions. Some of us are about as psychic as a brick but might have the ability to grow strong and healthy plants without any effort at all, while others can hold the attention of a hundred people in an open ritual at a festival and still manage to direct and focus the energy raised into a cone of power. Some of us are teachers, others are wood workers or craft persons, making altar plates, shaping and engraving staffs, creating jewellery, athames, carving runes or using a forge to make ritual swords. Bringing your everyday skills into your witching life and vice versa, helps us to make it into something concrete and solid, keeping it alive and a vital part of who we are and how we live in the real world, taking our path away from just being a 'Sunday' religion and turning it into something we really live every day.

I currently work in a very conventional office for a local government authority and as part of their commitment to employees, they offer four days of special leave on top of annual holidays to celebrate religious festival days that are not already covered by things like bank holidays and Christmas. It was something of an excitement to me to find out that Paganism, Druidry, Heathenry and Wicca are covered in the list of defined religions and so I duly booked time off for Samhain last year and my line manager, a Christian minister in his spare time, was happy to authorise it. By this time, my colleagues were already aware of my pagan faith so they understood – but it sparked another interesting conversion and one of them, a church-going Catholic, asked if it was really fair – after all, he did not get an extra four days leave. I explained that actually, he was entitled to them just as I was – there are plenty of holy days that some Catholics celebrate which fall outside of the days we already get off work in the form of bank holidays.

My desk at work has gradually accumulated a miniature altar – I have a tiny broom stuck to the corner of the monitor, an oak-gall from my favourite forest walk, a smoky quartz pyramid, some dried rowan berries and a tiny spiral with a couple of standing stones made out of blue tack. They aren't there for show – I use them, touch them, getting calmness to deal with awkward phone calls from the crystals, holding the oak-gall when I've been cooped all day and I'm starting to feel claustrophobic and the little broomstick serves to remind me that even if I'm full of stress and worry, my friends in the coven are just a phone call away and that as a witch, even if I'm on my own, I am never alone – the trees, the hills, the wind and rain and the ground beneath my feet connect me to the greater powers of the world, the Lord and Lady. I realise how lucky I am to be able to come out of the broom-closet at work, especially in such a conventional environment.

Our pagan choices and life style becomes more obvious in the home where we use our home-grown herbs to cook with and hang up bunches of dried lavender and rosemary. Sage and lavender braids or smudge bundles are lovely but can be expensive and drying out your own herbs is a good way of saving money, connecting to the elements in a very real way as you care for the plants, and bringing more a personal touch to your rituals. Growing your own herbs, fruits and vegetables is not for everyone but even a single potted plant on the window-sill is better than nothing and brings life into the home. Bedrooms can be filled with romantic candles that have an added benefit of a relaxing atmosphere that aids good sleeping patterns.

Being a witch is in the small things we do just as much as it is in the rituals, flowing capes and elaborate rhyming spells.

Having care and respect for our environment, being mindful of our thoughts and actions, offering pagan prayers and chants to celebrate the seasons and cycles of life are just a few of the small things we do that brings witchcraft and empowerment into our lives.

Aura Work

Working with spirit, energy, elementals and deity is one of the key practices I believe every witch should master and one of the starting points for this is learning to look after and sense the aura, the unseen energy body that we all have radiating out from our core.

There are hundreds of different opinions on exactly how many layers the aura has, what colours indicate a healthy aura and how the aura connects to the chakras etc. The one thing people do tend to agree on is that the aura can be a protective barrier against negative forces and unseen harmful energies and that when our aura is strong and healthy, it does the job quite well. However, if our aura is weak and sluggish, those same harmful or unwanted influences can be drawn to us.

Have you ever been in some public place, maybe on a crowded bus or queuing in a busy store, when you find yourself next to somebody who, for some reason you can't quite pinpoint, makes you feel suddenly uneasy and somehow unclean? The chances are that this person has unknowingly intruded on your sense of personal space and their aura is clashing with yours. Sometimes we can brush these encounters off lightly and carry on without giving it a second thought but sometimes it feels that we have somehow become tainted or dirtied by this brief contact and it can linger for hours, even days if we let it. A similar thing can happen when we've been through emotional turmoil – the aura is tainted with harmful emotions and it gets stuck. Where this unwanted energy has built up over time, people have become ill, sluggish, lacking in life force or vital energy. This is the kind of thing we can protect ourselves against with a bit of careful attention to our aura.

The aura can be seen or sensed by anyone who is sensitive to subtle energies – it can be seen in different layers, different colours, moving or static, sensed as a slightly magnetic-feeling presence by 'touching' it with your hands. Not everyone can see the aura though it's worth giving it a try – some people can't see it but can just 'feel' it. That's fine. There's no reason why everyone has to be able to see auras, after all. But still, it's definitely worth working on your own aura and it doesn't take long at all to carry out some cleansing and protection.

First of all, it's vital that you do some cleansing work as the last thing you want to do is build up that protective bubble and trap that tainted energy in with it. Cleansing is something you ought to do on a regular basis, using smudge bundles and a large feather to waft smoke around yourself, above you and below, behind and in front and visualising all the time that you are sweeping away anything that is harmful or negative. Using a singing bowl or a small bell is another way of doing it – hold the singing bowl or bell within your auric field in front of you and let it ring out with those sound vibrations shooing away negative energies. Try cleansing your aura or another person's in lots of different ways and see what works best.

One group I worked with on an informal basis some years ago lined everyone up in pairs facing each other, with people taking it in turns to walk down the centre. The first pair cleansed the aura, the next pair gently smoothed it, the next two buffed it and finally the aura was sealed by the last pair. My friend called it the aura car wash – I have no idea where she got the idea from but it worked brilliantly and everyone had fun working together.

Once your aura is spick and span clean, you can fill it up with positive, protective energy. This can been visualised (and when I say visualise, what I really mean is that you 'feel' it working very clearly) as a white, silver or gold stream of energy. We get this from above and below – stand tall and send your roots down in the ground, right into the earth – you know the drill by now – shoots spreading upwards to the skies, higher and higher up to the stars. Pull that energy down and into your centre, bring it up from the ground, focus clearly, don't imagine that you are doing this – know that you are doing this. Fill your aura up with positive, radiant energy from earth and sky and then seal it. Use your hands to direct that energy into a barrier all the way around you, above you and below you. It's said that the aura stretches out about as far as our outstretched hand, give or take a bit. Build up that cocoon to envelop you and seal in those beneficial vibrations of energy. Add an extra layer of protection by visualising the aura covered in a reflective surface, a little like a mirror, which repels and reflects away anything that would be harmful to you.

Empowerment

When we are fully empowered, we are feeling confident and self-assured, we are listening to carefully to what others say and being respectful, we are capable of being assertive and standing up for ourselves and others without being cocky. This kind of power is what I call empowerment, a power we possess within our deep self. It's not about being right or being better or being bossy, but about being capable and confident within ourselves. To lead a ritual and direct energy within it as well as keeping an eye on everyone else is not easy but it is very rewarding. As a priestess of many large rituals and small ones too, I know from experience that people are not easy to herd; we get distracted, we giggle amongst ourselves or squat down to tie shoe-laces when everyone else is raising their athames to the air elementals. Leading a bunch of pagans and witches in a ritual to create a cone of power takes skill and practice and the ability to laugh or cry while still bringing everyone back on track and to realise that it doesn't always matter if things don't go exactly as they were planned. This personal empowerment is important on an individual and personal level too, giving confidence and assurance when we have to deal with stressful, difficult or important situations and people.

If you've been planning a ritual for the sabbat and you're the one leading it, try to do an empowerment exercise beforehand. Often, in a close working group doing a ritual together, this can come to you through the rite of drawing down the moon or the sun. For other situations, if you can, try to do this just before you head into the event or at least as close to it as possible. Cleanse your aura and open your chakras and get yourself comfortable. Light a red candle for power and sit with your palms near its flame, close enough to feel its warmth. Absorb this warmth and let it soak into your skin while at the same time linking your roots to the ground and your shoots to the sky. Pull energy in from all three sources and into your body. Visualise the event ahead of you and see yourself clearly taking control of what you're doing there. See yourself speaking clearly and confidently, see yourself standing tall and smiling, enjoying the event and your place in it. Spend as long as you can with this image of yourself feeling confident, powerful, vibrant and strong all the time with this energy pouring into your spirit from the earth, from the sky, from the living flame in front of you. Draw a ball of energy up into your hands now, see it forming clearly and again imagine yourself at this event. Take that ball of energy and project it forwards to the self you see in front of you. Give it to yourself in the future, a ball of psychic confidence and empowerment that is now waiting for you to reach it in the future.

I am capable, strong and empowered, I am powerful, gifted and confident and everything runs smoothly. I am in my power.

When you are done, top up your aura with the warmth and energy of the candle flame and breathe deeply. Relax. When the event itself rolls around, be assured that you will pick up on that projected ball of empowerment that fuels you from within, confident and self-assured. Repeat the phrases again and feel that energy flooding through you.

> *I am capable, strong and empowered, I am powerful, gifted and confident and everything runs smoothly. I am in my power.*

Use the same kind of empowering exercise before a job interview, visit to the bank manager to re-mortgage, seeing a solicitor or when dealing with a hundred delegates at a business meeting. Make yourself a mojo bag in advance that you can carry around with you and fill it with things that make you feel strong – write down words like *strength, power, confidence,* on a piece of paper or charge a piece of hematite with strong, vibrant energy to put in the bag.

Sacred Journey

Deep journey or trance work is an important aspect of witchcraft that I find is often over-looked in favour of dressy rituals and spell craft or when it is touched upon, it's only the surface that gets uncovered in the form of guided meditation and visualisations but journey or trance, whichever you want to call it, can be an incredibly valuable implement in your witchy tool-kit. We enter a deeply relaxed state of mind and 'journey' with our psychic senses to another realm beyond this one where anything can happen. Here we can meet with archetypal figures such as the eternal mother and father, the god and goddess, the child, the wise elder woman, or we can meet and develop communications with our spirit guides and animal guides in journey. Similarly, we can meet with the anima/animus and with hidden aspects of our own psyche to gain insights, wisdom, stories, help and advice, ask for the solutions to problems or search our deep past to find out why we make the same mistakes over and over and use that information to decide how we can move past our blockages and develop more positive life patterns.

Deep journey work to visit the other realms, the Upperworld or the Underworld, rely on us being completely unaware of our physical selves and so deeply relaxed that our minds can shift into an altered state of consciousness, a state of trance. To be unaware of our bodies to this extent, we must be utterly comfortable and utterly relaxed. There are hundreds of relaxation and meditation CDs, drumming tapes and audio guides that can help you reach the state required for journey.

One good technique for relaxation which is pretty much guaranteed to work is what I call the rainbow countdown. It uses chakra colours but in waves, washing over the whole body from toes to head. Focus on the feelings that you would have if you lay on the beach and let waves wash slowly over you, bathing over you. Starting with red, see, feel and sense waves of colour washing over you from your toes and feet, up your lower legs, knees, thighs, over your hips and abdomen, washing up over your torso and covering your arms, shoulders and neck, washing like a gentle wave over your head. Each wave of red gradually changes to orange, the orange waves flow over you and change slowly to yellow, then green, blue, violet and finally white. This exercise should take around ten to fifteen minutes so you have plenty of time to let yourself relax that little bit deeper with every wave of changing colour, breathing out deeply at first then more slowly and finally not even being aware of your breathing at all – let it be completely natural and soft. When the green light washes over you, you should be so totally relaxed that you're barely aware of the surface you are lying on and by the time the white light reaches your head, you should feel like you are made of air, as light as a feather without weight or substance, completely and totally unaware of your body.

The place of power is one of the first places we visit in the other-worlds, an inner temple that we visit to start our journey. Plan ahead a little for this and figure out where you want that sacred space to be – you might want an outdoor temple on the beach with mountains in the background, a small clearing in a green woodland, by the side of a waterfall or the top of a high cliff with blue skies and not a cloud to be seen. Picture it clearly, the more detail you can come up with, the stronger the inner temple will be when you start your journeys.

So, having switched off from the mundane world through some deep meditation or relaxation technique, we now start to build our sacred space in the other realms. Visualise yourself standing at the edge of your inner temple and take in the scene, see the space as you want it to be and rub out anything you want to change – remember that this is going to be your starting point and also the place you return to at the end the journey. You need to recognise it, feel at home with it and associate the space as being yours. Walk into this sacred space and visualise there your altar with your working tools on it all set up just as you would have them in the physical world. If you want to, you can use them now to cast a circle around the boundary of your inner temple.

Spirit Guides

We all have guides whether you believe them to be the spirits of people who have passed over, a higher level entity from another plane or a construct of the imagination or hidden aspect of the self. Guides aren't always with us for ever, sometimes they move on and leave us in the care of a new guide – we may never know the reasons why – or we have a life-guide or master-guide who is always there while other guides pass into our lives for specific purposes. Your guide is here to help you, offer friendship, advice, guidance. Sometimes a guide chooses us while others might be assigned to us for a particular reason.

We can ask for our guides to make themselves known to us in the other realms and interact with them there safely though we are not forced to necessarily act on everything they say.

Just as we listen to the advice and opinions of our friends and then make our own decisions, we should do the same with our guides. They are there to do just that – to guide us. If we are prepared to follow blindly then we are giving them control over our lives and witchcraft is about being in control of our own lives ourselves, so do consider the words of wisdom your guide may offer but feel free to ignore it or use it as you see fit.

Enter your sacred space or inner temple as above and visualise a pathway that leads off and away and follow that path, leaving your temple space behind, and go along until you reach a small, pleasant area where you find a tall, healthy ash tree. Stand by the tree and ask for your guide to come forward to meet you. What happens next is not something that can be decided in advance, journeys like this are more personal, unique, unplanned and spontaneous than guided visualisations. Your guide may appear to you from behind the tree or right in front of you. She or he may be young, old, a child, a grandmother or a young man, the guide may be carrying something or could offer a hand-shake or a pat on the back as you greet each other. Talk to your guide and find out his or her name, don't feel under pressure to find out everything you want to know in this first session, you can come back another time to develop the friendship. Remember your manners, be respectful and thankful. This is a time to offer as well as take. Take plenty of time with this exercise and remember that this is your own, individual journey, there is no right or wrong. At any point during this journey or any other, you can return to your inner temple and back to your physical body. Remember that it's good manners to say thank you and wish them good-bye.

You can do more journeys in the same manner as this – to meet with your anima (men) or animus (women), to meet your spirit animal guide, to meet the Old Ones. You could journey to your inner temple and ask your guide to take you to a healing spring for emotional healing work: there you might see water elementals, undines or mermaids who comb your hair and sing you a healing chant. Take a journey to meet with the elemental guardians or spirits of each realm, again, you can ask you guide to take you to meet them or start in your place of power and follow a path that leads to a high mountain where the air spirits dwell or a deep cave to connect with earth elementals.

Returning

Coming back from journey work is fairly straight forward. Give thanks to your guide or whatever other being you have spent time with and make your way back to your sacred space on the inner planes. Sit calmly and reflect on your journey.

Breathe. Breathe. Be aware of your breathing. Be aware of your body, gradually feeling the sensation of your clothes against your skin, the chair you are sitting on. Be aware of your body. Breathe deeply a few times, start to shift yourself slightly, just move a small amount at first, gradually moving hands and arms, slowly, slowly coming to awareness of your physical surroundings. Open your eyes, sitting up when you feel like it. A glass of water and an apple or a piece of bread will do wonders for grounding you as will tapping your feet on the ground or shaking out your arms and legs. Grounding like this is important after deep journeys – it stops you from staying spaced out and walking round in a zombie-like daze afterwards and helps your thought processes clarify and examine what you've experienced. You can write your experiences of journey in your book of shadows if you keep one.

Anima and Animus

Tapping into the realms of the unconscious mind when we do any kind of spiritual work opens us up to the archetypes of our psyche and to the hidden parts, the unconscious mind, of our soul. As we develop our psychic, spiritual and intuitive senses archetypes often come to us in dreams and visions and offer insights and advice, a sensation of feeling whole and complete as we interact with them. Archetypes are symbolic forces that are separate from us and still a part of us – we have our conscious mind that we are aware of and the subconscious mind of which we are generally not. The animus is the masculine archetype of women and for men the anima is the female archetype. Being able to access that archetype opens up new levels of consciousness that offer inspiration, creativity and understanding.

Women connecting to the animus, related to the element of fire, can use it to come up with new solutions, decisiveness, strong thinking and reasoning. Fire is the realm of action, of getting things done, being motivated, intellectual thought, fiery power to move and act. For men, the anima, the water element, can give artistic solutions, creative flair, and sensitivity. Water offers balance, vision, full emotional feeling, intuitive thinking and empathy. Experiencing the anima/animus gives us a more complete understanding of women and men and how we think and feel in different ways and that understanding can help us relate better to others and build more solid and genuine friendships with the opposite gender. Similarly, not only can this understanding help us with others, it can help us to understand ourselves in different ways. It can shed some light on past actions and decisions we've made that seemed completely out of character and lets us realise that perhaps when we let our subconscious take over we are still in charge of our thoughts and not just dreaming or indulging in wishful fantasies.

We can connect to our anima or animus through deep journey work. Visit the sacred temple on the inner planes and ask your subconscious mind to meet you. They will be the opposite gender to yourself with qualities and personality traits that you probably won't recognise in yourself but this is a deep part of your mind and embracing that, accepting it and then integrating that part, is part of our journey as we strive to become more complete, whole and healthy. Ask your anima or animus what they have to tell you. What part of that archetype would benefit you most right now? What aspect of your hidden persona are you prepared to accept? How will you work in the physical realm to integrate that in your regular life?

Another way of listening to the anima/animus is through working with your dreams. Recording and interpreting dreams is something we often do on a fairly regular, or every morning, basis as we starting on the witching path but this dreaming is only the end product of our nightly wanderings – what about the beginning of that process? Years ago, after reading an amazing book which unfortunately I can't quite recall the name or author of, I had a go at programming my sleepy brain to dream about something specific and was surprised when it started to work. As I settled down to sleep I would tell myself over and over *tonight I shall dream about meeting my spirit guide (or whatever I was focusing on)* and after about a week it started happening pretty much the same as I had visualised it.

This worked brilliantly too when my daughter was having nightmares as a small child. Dreams are part of your imagination, I explained, and you can imagine anything you like in them so why not imagine that you have a good monster who comes to the rescue and scares away the bad monsters? She did this and it worked like a charm. Not only that, she then went on to become instinctively very good controlling her dreams. She would tell me that tonight, she'd like to dream about cute kittens, and sure enough in the morning that had been exactly what she'd dreamed of. We can do the same pre-programming any time we like with the intention of meeting our archetypal gender opposite and then recording and interpreting the experience in the morning.

CHAPTER 6

Whispers of Womanhood

The cycles we talk about most commonly in Wicca are the cycles of the year and of the moon. While the eight Sabbats and the monthly Esbats are certainly central to the Wiccan faith as acts of reverence, celebration and devotion to the spirit of nature, it's also important that we mark the significant cycles of our own, human lives. This is something that seems sadly lacking in our society – apart from Christenings, weddings and funerals, we have little to mark out and celebrate the turning points of our lives.

The familiar rites of passage for witches are the ceremony of Wiccaning, taking the place of the Christening service for new born babies; Hand-fasting, the ritual for a pagan wedding and the Requiem or memorial which is held as a funeral and wake for our Beloved Dead. Yet these are only three reasons to hold rites of passage to celebrate or acknowledge the changes and land-marks in our lives. We all have these phases to pass through; some of these are hard and painful, others easy and joyful. We undergo transformation, change, awakening, realisation, sorrow, joy, laughter and more with each major event that we go through in life.

From learning to walk and talk as a child to having your first signs of puberty to taking your first lover, your first relationship break-up to the coming of old age, getting your first job to seeing your first grey hair, we all have to deal with a lot of emotional, physical and spiritual stress throughout our lives. Some of the experiences we go through will bring us a tremendous amount of pain and heart-ache, some will leave us feeling worn-out but content, others still will make us ecstatic with love and pleasure. There are a multitude of milestones in our lives, many of which are glossed over, ignored or given a taboo status.

The transformative period from boy to man is often met with a challenge in which the boy becomes a man by spending three days and nights fasting on a hilltop to take part in his first battle as a warrior, thus proving his strength and bravery as a man. In countless fairy tales of yore, a girl becomes a woman by working for an older woman and only when she uncovers the secret of womanhood (often by uncovering a secret or opening a locked door) can she be free to live her own life. Tribal cultures that the western world considers primitive or indigenous often have very specific rites of passage or initiation ceremonies to mark the significant events in a person's life. Piercing, tattooing, scarification, circumcision and spirit journeys have all played their part in the initiatory traditions of various societies at different times.

In our society, such rituals are few and far between, sometimes thankfully so. There is definitely a place, however, for paying some kind of homage and honour to the cycles we pass through and it is hoped that paying attention to a handful of the occasions suggested here can guide you to the best way of marking the important events and times of transition in your own life, whatever they might be – even passing your driving test or graduation from university can be celebrated with a simple ceremony.

Some of the rituals given here for women concerning birth and pregnancy can also be useful for men as they support the women they love through these experiences. With a little imagination, the ritual outlines given here can be used in their entirety, changed to suit your needs or discarded completely if you want to write your own ritual. Witchcraft is a very personal faith and the first faith we must have is a strong, unshakable faith in our ability to practice it in a unique way that makes it wholly meaningful for the people concerned, whatever the books say!

Women have often been referred to as the weaker sex. Any woman will tell you that this phrase was coined by a man who has never known a woman when she has been truly in her power! Women are magical – they hold the ultimate power and responsibility – that of growing and birthing children. Women have to be physically healthy and strong to go through pregnancy and birth. With the monthly menstrual flow, women also have to be strong as that can bring its own problems – problems most women would rather not have to deal with. Women give strength through endlessly supporting their loved ones, families, friends and children. To say that women are weak is demeaning and meaningless. Women are strong and powerful, with important gifts to offer the world.

Some women are abused, forced into demeaning jobs, work as full-time and yet unpaid child-minders, are often given the role of domestic slave and treated with unkindness in so many ways that it beggars belief and still a woman can come up for air and start again with a single-minded determination and utter belief in her ability to get through it, to break-away and start over again. Other women are treated with reverence, loved and rewarded, showered with gifts, paid homage to by their men and acknowledged for their great sacrifice to others. Women can be hard-headed business-leaders, artists and scientists and still be good at all kinds of other things too.

The rites of passage for women can focus on any aspect of womanhood. Women can use their moon-blood for sacred rituals – a blood sacrifice without wounding. The cycles of womanhood are not only about menstruation and pregnancy however, they are also about puberty, pregnancy, miscarriage, birth, motherhood, the menopause and death among other things. The transition from girl to woman is not always an easy time and the challenge of motherhood does not always come naturally to the new mother, irrespective of how much she has looked forward to and planned for the birth of her child. Becoming a lover for the first time, giving birth, suffering a miscarriage or even making the hard decision to end a pregnancy, becoming a grandparent, going through puberty and the menopause, seeing our children have families of their own. All of these unique events take their toll on women and there is very little, or more often a complete lack of, acknowledgement or reward.

Some of the most important things that happen in a woman's life are overlooked or taken as matter of course and treated as something to be brushed under the carpet or forgotten about entirely. Women are powerful, life-giving, beautiful creatures. Reclaim the joy of honouring all your cycles with ritual and celebration.

Puberty

The onset of menstruation, known as the Menarche, brings with it an exciting time for a young girl but it can also be a frightening and worrying time. Any group of pre-pubescent girls will discuss the subject earnestly – unfortunately a lot of the information they gain through rumour and gossip is ill-informed, inaccurate and contradictory. Some of the stories passed down can fill a young girl with feelings of absolute dread and there are so many questions without clear answers. *How much will I bleed? Is it painful? How long does it last? When will I start? How will I know?* Because menstruation varies so much from woman to woman, they will never truly know the answers to until they experience it first hand for themselves. If you are a mother, you already have the experience needed to prepare your daughters as fully as you can for their own menarche and will hopefully do so in plenty of time to try alleviate some of their worst fears.

To make the transition from girlhood to womanhood easier, many cultures have special rituals for the onset of puberty and the menarche. Some rites of passage are of great significance to the girls involved while others are unpleasant or even abusive. Fortunately, there also are plenty of ceremonies and rites of passage with are full of honour and respect.

Rituals for a young woman can include seclusion from the rest of the tribe or clan as the other women gather round her, giving red coloured gifts, special foods, songs and ritual dance. Pagan women sometimes give their own daughters special gifts that have been passed down through the female blood line or some gift they have hand-made for the special occasion; other girls receive advice, wisdom and insights into womanhood from the female tribal elders.

When we held a ceremony for my friend's daughter some years ago when she reached her menarche, about twenty of us gathered, all women including some of her teenage friends. We told stories, there was a feast and music and dancing. She was bestowed with gifts and kisses and hugs. Now that young girl has grown up to be a woman with a child of her own. It was a deeply moving experience to be there in support of a young woman who was just starting her journey towards adulthood and it was also a great opportunity for the women of our Pagan community to gather and share our own menarche stories.

The menarche, or first period, is the sign most girls and women recognise as being the single most important factor in the phase of puberty. Having periods is something, as already said, that can cause a great deal of apprehension for months or years prior to it actually happening. When the big event finally arrives, and frank discussion with your own women friends will bear this out, there is often a sense of it being somewhat of an anti-climax. Nothing changes outwardly; nobody cares or even knows that you've had your first period. The days pass as they always have done and life continues in more or less the same manner as before. Regardless of life carrying on, this girl has fully entered her phase of becoming a woman and it can almost be a disappointment, especially if it comes hand-in-hand with pains and aches and teasing or bullying from her peers.

As most of us have no acknowledgment or honouring of puberty for the young women in our lives, we have the opportunity to create something magical and unique and give them support and recognition in their transition time with a gift, a celebration and a ritual of initiation. Help your daughters and your young women friends to acknowledge and feel proud of this transformation and let them know it is something to be celebrated.

Ritual for the Menarche

Preparations can include making or choosing something – a new gift or family heirloom – to pass on to her. Put this gift and one red and one black cloak or sheet on the altar, which should be draped in red with red candles and a statue or symbol of the maiden goddess. Food offerings and background music can, and indeed should, be chosen by the girl herself, as it is her celebration. She might like to have some of her friends present or might not want a ritual at all – it could simply be too embarrassing, after all! If she decides to go ahead, this ritual can be adapted to include anything else she and/or you feel is appropriate.

Designate someone to act as Priestess for the rite. The dialogue can be adapted as necessary. The girl's hands should be red with body-paint or henna. Above all, remember that all the rituals provided in this book *can* be used exactly as they are if you like, but they are only ideas and the benefits will be greater if you make them unique to you in some way or alter it altogether. Go with whatever feels natural for you and make the ritual as spectacular or as simple as you please.

Cast the sacred circle as you would normally and invoke the goddess in her maiden aspect as a young woman of innocence and purity. The Priestess should be covered with the black cloak and the red one is set on the altar.

Pick up the gift and show it to the girl. Ask her if she is ready to receive the gift of womanhood. She should, of course, say yes. Replace the gift on the altar and ask her if she is ready to undertake a challenge in order to receive it. Again, she responds by saying yes.

Priestess: *I am the goddess of Old. I am the one who sees all, knows all and is all. I am the truth behind the face of all women; I am the light behind her eyes. I give you a riddle. Are you willing to answer it?*

Girl: *I am ready.*

Priestess: *I am beholden to no-one but the tides of life. I am always beautiful, even when I have no beauty. I am swaying, dancing, powerful and magical. I am an object of passion and desire. I am hard-working and my life is not always easy. I am powerful in my sorrows and pains. I am the dancer in the face of music, I am the strong-heart in the soul of Mankind, I am the dream of all. What am I?*

Girl: *You are a woman. (Priestess removes the black cloth and lays it on the floor)*

Priestess: *You are young; you have no experience of these matters. Show me a sign that you are ready for the challenge of womanhood.*

Girl: (Holds hands up) *I have the mark of womanhood on my body. I am ready to face the challenge of womanhood.*

Priestess: *Then kneel, daughter of the goddess, that I may give you rebirth as a woman.* (The girl kneels on the black cloth and is covered completely by the red. If anyone else is present, they should join in the chant and circle around the girl.)

All *Bold, strong, powerful woman.*
Nurturing, loving, caring woman.
Magical, powerful, beautiful woman.
You are the maiden goddess made woman.
You are the Maiden, You are the Maid.

Priestess: (Removes the red cloth) *Rise up, daughter of the goddess.* (The girl stands) *I offer you this gift as a symbol of your womanhood. Keep it always and honour the cycles of the goddess in your life.* (The gift exchanges hands) *You are a Woman.*

The Priestess can lead everyone round in a spiral or circle dance to the chosen music and encourage the group to raise energy to bless the girl. As the energy starts to peak, raise it up with the hands as high as it can go and then let it shower down to give her the energy and ability to cherish the first real sign of her transition to womanhood.

At this point, the elements and deity should be given thanks before any feasting and the circle should be closed with a great whooping shout. If there are several teenaged girls present, this is the point at which the adults can retire to the kitchen for coffee while the girls have their private party and celebration.

Pregnancy – Motherhood

Becoming pregnant, for the most part, is a wonderful, joyful thing and every woman who has felt the stirring of a baby in her womb knows both how vulnerable and how powerful it can make her feel. However, pregnancy is not an easy time, even when things run smoothly. The first three months bring the initial joy of a confirmed pregnancy and then morning sickness might visit us not just in the morning but noon and night as well. The second three months mean we say goodbye to size ten jeans and find out more about how the baby is developing at ante-natal classes which tell us what to expect during the actual birth but do far too little to prepare women for the experience of actually looking after a child. Finally, the third trimester gives way to fear of the birth itself, frantic planning of what the little one will wear and whether you should breast or bottle-feed and the enthusiastic but often unwelcome need of other people – including complete strangers when you're going about your normal daily business – to intrude on your space by patting your stomach to feel the little kicking of the unborn child. As a woman's pregnancy makes itself known, it seems to make her public property and this can be very intrusive for the mother-to-be. The birth itself is at once a worrying and delightful time and a woman has a wide range of emotions concerning it, not to mention the physical onslaught of labour.

There are few things that warm the heart quicker than a new-born babe and friends and family hasten to the bed-side, congratulating the mother and cooing over junior. Baby is showered with kisses and gifts and cards galore and visitors are full of questions about baby. Mother is by now exhausted, overjoyed, in pain, feeling vulnerable, overwhelmed, wanting quiet time with her partner and their new baby. Very little is done to nurture her, to take time to listen to her and honour her wishes when the focus is on the baby's cute dimples or soft wisps of fine hair. Wiccan baby naming ceremonies have been dealt with time and again and Wiccaning events are becoming popular but once again, the focus is almost entirely on the baby.

This ritual, performed shortly before or after birth, is designed solely for the mother, to help her consolidate the highly charged emotions she has been experiencing ever since she decided to have a baby and to acknowledge her new role of motherhood.

To prepare for this ritual it is helpful to have a baby-minder if the mother has already given birth. This doesn't mean baby can't be held or breast-fed as the ritual is carried out, but it does ensure that the ritual can still concentrate on the new mother if baby needs attention and she wants to maintain her focus. The altar should be decorated with a white cloth, fresh flowers, a long, white ribbon and a glass of milk. Have a large pile of soft cushions, an easy chair or bean bags in the centre of the working space and make the room as beautiful and comfortable as possible; use gentle background music, candles, incense etc., to enhance the calm and relaxed atmosphere.

The Ritual

If at all possible, everything should be done by someone other than the mother unless stated otherwise. If this is not practical, the new mother can either play two roles, the supporter and herself, or can implement changes to the ritual if she prefers. Start the ritual with the mother outside the circle.

A supporter or Priestess should cast the circle and invoke the elements, the god and the goddess in her Mother aspect. The new mother is now invited into the circle through a door which is then closed behind her. Lead her to sit comfortably in the centre of the circle and the first Priestess takes the flowers and lays them at the mother's feet.

1st Priestess: *I offer these flowers to you, valued mother, that you may grow in your role of motherhood. As flowers spring forth with the energy of the earth, so may you be filled with the energy and vitality you need for your life as a mother.*

The second Priestess then brings the glass of milk to her, which she accepts and places beside the flowers.

2nd Priestess: *I offer you this milk, a symbol of mothering and of nourishment. May you always receive the physical, spiritual and emotional nourishment and support that you need to fulfil your new role as a mother.*

The mother herself should now lay back and relax, as one of her supporters leads her into the following visualisation. Make sure she is comfortable and warm. If baby is present, she can choose to feed and cuddle him throughout the visualisation or pass him to the minder so that she can fully focus on herself.

1st Priestess: *You are surrounded by a white mist, the mist is all around you, and you feel warm and comfortable. The mist is warming and shades of light, yellow, orange and gold become visible. The light source is coming closer and you are completely at ease and comfortable. The light changes gradually, taking form, the form of a woman. She is heavy with pregnancy and swelling breasts. The mother goddess stands before you, smiling. Her eyes are kind and caring, you are bathed in their light; it touches your skin, making you feel cherished and nurtured. Lift your hand to the goddess. She takes your hand and kneels beside you. Let her breathe the breath of warmth and love on your skin as she kisses your brow. The mother goddess can offer wisdom, advice and insights. Ask your questions of her; ask if there is anything she can tell you that will benefit you now.*

A short interval

1st Priestess: *Give your thanks to the mother goddess for the advice she has offered and for the gift of motherhood. She begins to draw away, still smiling, still warm. The golden light fades to orange and slowly to yellow. The white mist is returning and you can feel yourself gradually come back to the here and now. When you are ready, open your eyes and slowly sit up.*

The mother takes the glass of milk and drinks it, giving thanks. The white ribbon is now laid out on the floor near the circle's perimeter. It is a symbol of purity and rebirth.

1st Priestess: *You are child of the mother goddess; she bestows on you the gift of motherhood. As a mother you will have joy and pain, pleasure and disappointment, excitement and anxiety. Are you ready for the challenge of motherhood?*

Mother: *I am ready.*

2nd Priestess: *Your baby will grow into a child and through to adulthood and will need your care and attention for much of this time and your love throughout it all. Will you promise to love your child through all of these phases?*

Mother: *I give my promise.*

1st Priestess: *A baby needs a mother who is strong, full of life and vibrancy. Do you promise to nurture yourself, to look to your own needs to ensure you can meet those of your baby?*

Mother: *I give my promise.*

2nd Priestess: *We invite you to cross the threshold, the barrier between your life now and your life as a mother. As you leave the sacred circle, you become one with the mother goddess as you become a mother yourself. We treasure the sacred gift of motherhood within you. Blessed Be.*

The mother can now cross the ribbon and leave the circle, acknowledging the support and gifts she has received and feeling uplifted by her brief consort with the great mother of all.

The supporters should now close the circle and tidy the space, giving thanks to the elements, the goddess and god and leaving an offering of wine and fruit to the Old Ones.

When Things Go Wrong

There are very few, if any, satisfactory explanations for why miscarriages happen and even the best explanation of the medical terms involved will not address the only question that really needs to be answered: *'Why?'* There will never be anything that would make it easier to bear.

Women who suffer miscarriage are often subjected to harsh, unpleasant medical procedures and the clinical staff who can do little to ease their physical and emotional pain. It all too distressing to hear about cases of miscarriage in which the women who lose their babies are treated in an off-hand, matter-of-fact manner by doctors and nurses who's best advice is to 'wait three months and try again'.

When a woman has spent the last year or the last ten trying for a baby, when a woman has been heart-broken with each period that meant she wasn't pregnant, when a woman has been planning her pregnancy for months or years only to suffer a miscarriage, it is easy to think she has been abandoned by the gods. She might feel guilty about some trivial thing she has done or imagined she has done that might have caused it, she might be frightened of future miscarriages and because there is very rarely a body to bury, there is no funeral, no ceremony, no chance to say goodbye. This is probably one of the hardest things about losing a baby. It is intended that all women - and men - who feel the unexpected loss of their baby, for whatever reason and no matter how long ago or how recent the loss, can carry out a ritual like this one to help them to move on.

Loss of Pregnancy Ritual

For someone who has lost a baby, the emotions can be too raw and fragile to focus on ritual and preparations are of necessity minimal. It would be useful to have a partner or friend present to support you. It would not be appropriate to suggest words here, as the reasons for the pregnancy loss are as varied as are the emotions involved, any words given would be without meaning; rituals this deep and hard come straight from your soul. Speak from your heart or compose something in advance to read out. If you have any scan photographs of the baby, put these on the altar. You may want to have a token gift to bury in the garden as an offering to the spirit of the baby – a small toy or pair of booties, for instance. If so, the ritual can be done outside to include this symbolic burial.

Create your sacred space as you normally would, invoking the five elements. Invoke the moon goddess in her crone aspect and the god as the dark lord of the forest.

Address the Old Crone directly in the centre of the circle and use your own words to tell her how you feel about your loss. Speak to the dark god, say the words that come to you. Be honest with your words, say whatever feels right at the time. This is between you and the gods, if you think they have abandoned you, scream it out at them. Emotions do us no good when kept deep inside.

If your partner is with you, you can read together a meaningful poem or simply hold each other and cry. Let out all that raw, painful emotion.

If you are able to, look at your scan photographs and treasure the memory of the tiny baby, smile and be glad that it filled your heart with joy, even if only for a brief moment. Think about the spirit of the baby and wish it well, send it your love and ask that it is taken care of and loved.

If you want, you can visit the realms of journey and ask your guide if you are able to speak with the spirit of your unborn child. If the spirit is free to do so, it is likely to come to you. If the spirit cannot come to you, this could be because it is doing other work in the spirit realms or it could be incarnating somewhere else; ask your guide to tell you.

Ask any questions you want to and tell your baby's soul how much you love it and wanted it to be your baby. It is believed that the spirit of the unborn child can sometimes incarnate with you fully in the future, ask if this will be possible.

It can be a powerfully healing experience to meet with the spirit and say goodbye in this way. By meeting with the spirit and getting any insights into the situation it might be able to offer, you will be able to fully recognise that this was not your fault.

Say goodbye to the baby's spirit and be glad that you met each other, even if only in journey.

When you have done and said everything you wanted to in order to say goodbye to your baby, start to gather yourself together and close the ritual space. Say hale and farewell to the goddess and god but there is no need to give thanks; on this occasion, you may well feel as though there is nothing to thank them for.

For a priestess or priest who is asked to carry out a ritual for someone else, the above format can still be used and the grieving couple can add to it as necessary. Once again, there is no right or wrong - when it comes to pagan rituals the beauty of each ceremony is in its uniqueness and meaningfulness to the people involved.

Becoming a Crone

The menopause is not generally given much importance – if people talk about it all, they talk about hot-flushes, greying hair and the end of fertility. The menopause is a sign of ageing in women and getter older in itself can be hard to deal with in a world full of supermodels, face-lifts, botox, slimming pills and *'now-covers-all-grey!'* hair-dye. Becoming old is something the average woman is not eager to embrace and we are pressured into looking amazing at all times, just like the mature celebrity women who advertise hair colour or moisturisers. A look at her deep laughter lines or salt-and-pepper hair will soon tell you the truth about a woman's age, although these days there are plenty of things which can hide, delay, though not entirely diminish, the effects of ageing.

Feared throughout many cultures, the goddess in her aspect of crone is thought of as the reaper, the bringer of death. She is the one who cuts the thread of life while her sister fates spin and measure it. The old crone is also the old wise woman who sits at the bottom of a tree or in a dark cave waiting for people to visit her lair and hear her secrets. Having seen all of life, the old woman has secrets indeed and can give these out if she is feeling generous.

How will you be as you become a crone? Old and feeling it or old and feeling young? Role-models of older women in the public eye may look graceful, elegant or glamorous. Mature actresses and celebrities may appear to have flawless skin and vibrant hair colour but you can bet your hat they use hair-dye and wear a covering of heavy make-up to make themselves look that good; their laughed-in wrinkles will give them away next time you look properly.

It is the real women elders in our lives who can be role-models for us – think of someone you know who inspires you. The energetic granny who takes on a part-time university course or the eighty-year old lady who continues to use public transport, do her own laundry and smiles every day without fail – these are the real women who can be our inspiration as we grow wiser and older. As I look at my own mature women friends, I realise how truly beautiful they all are and how much I value the insights, wisdom and knowledge they pass on as a result of their long, rich lives. These women, the ones who look like they know something you don't, have had their hearts broken in their youth, had children or grandchildren being sick in their laps, they have watched their hair turn grey and had their share of laughter and tears. These amazing women provide much more valuable role models than the celebrity glamour-grans. They can be our inspiration for growing old either gracefully or disgracefully, depending on your preference.

Becoming old doesn't have to be frightening; mature women can still wear make-up, go to the gym, take on a new career, have fun, travel the world, have sex and excitement and more. It has often been said that keeping active helps to keep you young and there really is a lot of truth in this. Grab hold of the menopause, yank it past you and accept your croning time as your way of becoming a Wise Woman of the World.

Celebrating the Laughing Crone

The following poem is a ritual in itself, giving you a new identity, confirming the wisdom and wonders of maturity. Invite all your friends to join you as you celebrate your menopause and the coming of (old) age. Plan your ritual to include the gifts you want to receive or ask your friends choose something appropriate. Put a bowl full of rose petals on the altar along with an image of how you want to be in your third age. To begin the ritual, you might like to wear a black shawl and cast this off after saying the poem, accepting with the gesture that old age can be bright and colourful and as you grow and age you can choose to embrace the light in your life.

The only thing that is really important in the ritual is to keep the focus on the positive aspects of aging; if we dwell too much on negative images, they can become our expectations and as we know, the universe is always ready to fulfil our expectations, good or bad!

Create a sacred circle and invoke the crone goddess and the horned god and recite this poem or a similar one. This even has a bit of sing-song feel to it so you could try a few run-throughs to see if you can make it work as a chant.

I am an old woman,
I am a wise woman,
I am a teacher,
A woman of the earth.
I am an old woman,

I am a wise woman,
I am a healer,
A woman of the sky.
I am an old woman,
I am a wise woman,
I am a secret-keeper,
A woman of the sun.
I am an old woman,
I am a wise woman,
I am a portent,
A woman of the sea.
I am an old woman,
I am a wise woman,
I am a Goddess,
The beauty of all life.

Your friends can take turns to shower you with rose petals and offer you a gift, such as wisdom, maturing with style, the gift of laughter or a healthy sex-life.

Close the circle and have a cackle and a feast with your treasured women friends. You could make this ritual more elaborate – perhaps creating an archway to walk through to symbolise the passage of time, with flowers and white drapes and confetti to be showered over you as you emerge.

The Goddess Within

The stereo-typical image of a woman is that of mother, carer and nag. The commercial image of women is strikingly beautiful, not very intelligent and painfully thin. The reality of women is that they can be all of these things and a combination of many more. Women are the embodiment of the goddess and in order to recognise yourself as such, a journey is suggested here to attune yourself to your feminine power and strength. Although journey is normally inspired and spontaneous, there is a certain value to reading a premeditated formula beforehand to give ideas about what can or will happen when you journey for a particular purpose. This journey is offered as a way of leading you to the right kind of events to acknowledge what it means to be the embodiment of the goddess, not as a script that must be strictly adhered to.

Prepare a comfortable place to lie down for a good half-hour or so and make as sure as you can that you won't be interrupted for the duration.

Cleanse your space and cast a circle, invoking the elements, goddess and god in the normal manner. Carry out a deep relaxation exercise in whatever way is easiest for you and begin to slowly slip into your state of journey.

Begin in your place of power and look around to see how it is today. If your journey self is wearing clothes, remove them now and stand naked and bold in your special place. Ask for the goddess to come to you and wait for her to appear. Notice which direction she comes from, East, South, West or North. Perhaps she comes up from the ground or descends from the sky. Is she alone or accompanied by her companion animals?

When the goddess comes to you, kneel in reverence and wait for her to signal to you before you stand again. Notice which aspect she is currently in and ask her to tell you the secrets of this aspect. She will appear to you as maiden, mother and crone at once or in turn, telling you the secrets of each aspect and how you can fully understand what they mean in your life. The goddess will speak with both positive and negative messages, she is not always to be loved and sometimes we fear her darkness and her death-bringing. She is the one who has birthed the stars and all of the world is under her gaze.

As you speak with her and she tells you the tales of womanhood that you need to understand, notice how she appears. Does she remain in one aspect or change, shifting from one to the next? Is she as benevolent as you assumed she would be? Are there hidden depths in her eyes?

Ask the goddess how you can integrate the knowledge she has given you. Ask her the secrets of your heart; tell her your worries and concerns. Let her smooth your hair and whisper in your ear. When you think it is appropriate, ask the goddess if you can become one with her and let her radiance wash over you. Let her envelop you completely and smother you with the glorious sensation of being a goddess. The goddess is woman, with all her amazing qualities. Feel the buzz of energy and the vibrations of the goddess running through all of you – mind, body and soul. Ask her to leave a part of this feeling within you as she leaves and she will start to withdraw and depart from your sacred space. Give thanks, a simple smile or a heartfelt word.

Slowly look around you now, with your goddess eyes. See your place of power and notice if anything has been changed or appears to you differently. Stand tall and proud and speak out loud:

'I am strong and powerful, I am a Woman, I am the Goddess.'

Begin to make your way back to the surface of consciousness and return slowly to the real world. Write down your journey experience and the secrets you have learned from the goddess. Have something to eat and drink to ground yourself.

Give thanks to the goddess and god and the elements and close your circle.

CHAPTER 7

Mysteries of Manhood

Men are brave and tough; they are stronger and more aggressive than women, aren't they? Men are decisive, bold and fearless – right? In some respects, yes, but men are also vulnerable, caring, emotional or fearful. Trying to live up to the bravado and tough talk of what men 'should' be is becoming increasingly harder for today's man. Boys are automatically pushed towards playing with cars and guns, told they must be brave and not cry when they are hurt or upset. As they grow up, boys learn that letting their feelings show is a sign of weakness or effeminacy. When boys become men they are told that it is okay to cry after all – the 'new man' has arrived on the scene and completely contradicts the teachings of a generation.

Whichever image a man identifies with, the horned god is one of the archetype who can cover it all. The horned god is both the hunter and the hunted. As the hunted, he is the stag – a wild, free and untamed spirit, a sensory, virile and powerful expression of life. The hunter is the provider – courageous, strong, decisive, well trained and disciplined. Classical Greek teachings of the goat-footed god Pan, from whose name we get the word pandemonium, describe him as a creature full of joy, sexual and sensual, playful and content, strong and self-confident. Both Pan and the horned god seem to be good role models for men to aspire to; emotional and courageous, playful and natural.

Another archetype to consider is that of the Wise Man, old Greybeard, the shamanic guide or grey haired elder, leaning on his staff as he teaches the mysteries and wisdoms of manhood and life to the young boys who are about to reach manhood. The wise man can be seen as the provider of maturity, imparting knowledge and information regarding the roles and responsibilities a man might be expected or encouraged to take on to support his community and family.

There are several stereotypical images of men which are just plain sexist or unfounded in reality. While stereotypes have to start somewhere and may contain elements of truth, the whole of the truth is much deeper and more profound; belittling and snide comments about men and masculinity, often made by women bearing a grudge or in unhappy relationships, serve only to highlight the negative things that one person has done instead of acknowledging that we *all* have the ability to act in ways that are detrimental to ourselves and to others, whether we are male or female.

The traditional image of the male hunter shows a strong, instinctive man who hunts to provide for his family; a traditional role of the male warrior is seen again as strong and proudly fighting to protect his family, tribe or country; men who are gay are often wrongly thought of as being weaker and more feminine than heterosexual men and any man who shows his emotions freely is also seen in the eyes of society on the whole as weak and effeminate. Identifying with a positive male role model, one who is strong and sensitive, decisive and considerate, might prove to be a valuable asset to men and boys.

Often it seems as though women are obsessed with discussing men's less endearing qualities, female office gossip consists of little else for the majority of the time; one office I worked in a few years ago was an open plan office of around forty-five women with nearly all of them griping and sniping about how *all men are the same, men don't clean the house, men always forget anniversaries, all men are useless.* All of them? Really? If they are so unhappy with their husbands and boyfriends, why stay in the relationship instead of moving on and letting him go so that he can find someone who appreciates him? I am very thankful that despite coming from a very difficult relationship herself, my mother taught me that it's people, not men or women, who can be all of those awful things – the actions of one person do not represent the actions of the many. I appreciate how lucky I am with my dear husband who is the most patient and loving man in the world – so what if he doesn't hoover as often as I do? There are many other things he does do very well where I stumble and fail. Women could be celebrating the positive things about the men they love and about men in general. Men are magnificent, strong, powerful and sensitive beings and need to be respected as such, rather than being criticised for any failings they might have as individuals – we all have shortcomings and unhelpful character traits, regardless of our gender.

Today's men still come under a lot of pressure to provide for and protect the family unit, even in cases where the family unit consists of two men living together as a couple and in relationships where a woman earns the higher wage. The urge to provide safety and security for loved ones stems back to the times when our male ancestors were the hunters and the females had babies and looked after the home. Of the two sexes, few would argue that men in general tend to be physically stronger than women and there is a natural logic in sending the strongest people of the tribe or clan out to hunt wild animals but we have moved on and our attitude as a society finally seems to moving on too but the instincts often remain.

Many of the men I've spoken to find that there is no safe way for them to express these protective instincts and this can be detrimental to their psychological well-being. These are natural, instinctive urges to protect the family and provide security, which need to find an outlet or be cooped up without expression and risk coming out as depression, stress, anger or aggression directed in an inappropriate manner.

While it wouldn't be healthy for men to go out and have a fight every night just to satisfy their inner hunter, this is nevertheless what we seem to be experiencing in our cities and towns every Friday or Saturday night after too many pints – a signal, perhaps, that men are letting out their defensive and hunting instincts in an irrational, illogical way that serves no positive purpose for anyone involved. One way out of this situation is to provide a safe and reliable way to use that physical strength and adrenaline productively. What are the circumstances that provide this safe outlet? Martial arts are one good way of utilising the more aggressive male instincts in a safe environment. Other sports such as running, rowing or cycling for example, could also be useful as tools in providing a safe outpouring of the physical energies involved with the urge to fight and protect.

Men are seen as strong emotionally too; it is still very much frowned upon in mainstream society for men to express emotions like love or anger and especially fear or sadness or depression. Men and boys who give way to fear or sadness by crying are often picked on or bullied with taunts, name calling or worse. However, men do have these feelings just as women do, although it may be harder for them to admit it. The real weakness comes not from venting those emotions but from holding them inside through fear or lack of understanding and support. Keeping a tight rein on their feelings may give others the impression that they can cope with difficulties easily, but it can lead to a building up of unexpressed feelings that are often left simmering below the surface in an unhealthy manner. Men's support groups are springing up in the pagan community that give an opportunity for men to come together to express themselves.

Some of the men I've spoken to found that they had a long wait between the onset of puberty and the time they first realise that they had become a man, rather than being a boy or youth. Manhood is not always easily obtained and encompasses much more than mere physical maturity; it concerns the ego, self-esteem and the admiration or respect of others, responsibility and emotional maturity. There are several situations or events that seem to help affirm the coming of manhood, falling in love for the first time, the first relationship break-up, achieving success in particular skills, fatherhood, gaining levels of responsibility career progression and so on.

There are very few rites of initiation for men in today's world to honour these different phases and while there are groups who try and focus on the rituals and ceremonies concerning men-only mysteries, research by a female author indicates that a lot of male mystery groups and individual men are of the opinion that the greatest mystery for men is women and how to deal with them and group discussions often revolve around this eternal conundrum.

Puberty

Rites of passage into manhood across the world have variously included adult and childhood circumcision, drug induced shamanic journeys to meet with a guide or mentor, challenges, tests of endurance, getting tattoos of status or being involved for the first time in the male-oriented rituals of a tribe. For today's man, the rituals below are intended as a guide on which to base more personal rites of passage, offered in the hope that all men everywhere can honour their wonderful masculinity and live as freely as possible while accepting and acknowledging all aspects of their manhood.

The most obvious outward sign of male puberty is the voice breaking but this is the sign of maturity that young women, rather than young men, tend focus on. The rise in testosterone levels of a young man will be much more important to him and can cause concern, aggression or embarrassment in a variety of situations. Another clear sign of puberty in young men is, of course, the ability to have regular erections and to ejaculate; even though they have known intellectually what was going on, some men have described their first experience of a full ejaculation as somewhat of a surprise when it actually happens. Encounters with pretty young girls for a boy going through puberty must be excruciatingly difficult at times and young men appear to be, on the whole, somewhat unprepared for the embarrassing event of untimely erections. Perhaps there is a need for more frank discussions and accurate information to be made more readily available to boys in the run up to puberty. Reliable sources of information regarding male puberty are not openly discussed for boys and playground or peer group gossip about puberty won't always be correct, much as we've seen is the case for young girls. Puberty seems to be a taboo subject, hardly even glossed over in passing conversation. Men (and women) have a responsibility to teach their sons about puberty and all it entails but most father and son relationships have not offered the same frankness or depth of information and advice that many girls get from their mothers about the effects and concerns of puberty.

If a young man can be helped through these times with a sensitive, yet not intrusive, older man acting as guide and mentor, the whole experience can be made easier to deal with and to understand. A ritual to acknowledge the changes he goes through might also prove worthwhile to a young man if he is supported through life with Pagan or Wiccan parents. It would be easier and less embarrassing to carry out any rituals specifically for this time with an all-male cast.

This ritual is a staged fight between two warriors, with the young man acting as challenger to the elder. In preparation for the ritual, plan the moves and techniques that will be used to stage the fight, which must be choreographed to make sure everyone knows what they are supposed to do. Encouragement should be given to the young man to think or meditate on the responsibilities and attributes, both positive and negative, that manhood will bring to him. A gift appropriate to manhood and responsibility can be chosen by the boy's father or other male elder.

The ritual should be done out of doors for preference, allowing plenty of space and as many men as possible are to join in the ceremony for support and encouragement. Swords and shields can be made out of stiff cardboard and covered in silver foil for effect. Preparing these in advance as a group will be a good opportunity for frank discussions about male matters.

Challenge of the Warrior

Place weapons, shields, helmets and armour inside the circle and have the attending men divided into two groups to support either the young or old warrior. To begin with, have both warriors unarmed.

The old warrior should be surrounded by his attendants and the young man, the challenger, should approach with his friends following him. The circle can be cast as normal, invoking the god as the Celtic warrior Bran or the Norse god Odin.

Challenger: Who is the leader of this tribe?

Warrior: *I am* (name), *a great warrior and leader of the tribe. Who are you?*

Challenger: *I am (name) and I am a greater warrior than you have ever been...*

Warrior: *A warrior? You are but a boy, not yet tested in battle.*

Challenger: *And you are old, you are worn out and past your prime. This tribe needs a new leader and I am he. I am stronger and younger than you, old man. Dare you fight me?*

Warrior: *Of course I dare. Arm yourself if you think you can beat me.*

Challenger and warrior now dress up in silver tunics and arm themselves with the weapons. A carefully staged fight should ensue, taking care not to actually harm anyone but nevertheless the old warrior is to be symbolically beaten and fought to the ground. The attending men should egg on one side or the other, clapping, cheering and shouting – make it light-hearted and fun.

Warrior: *I am dying! You have beaten me, boy.*

Challenger: *Call me Boy no longer, I have become a man*

Attendant: *Come forward, brave warrior, and accept the mantle of responsibility you have rightfully earned.*
(He hands over the gift).

Challenger: *I claim this token of responsibility and accept my place as leader and warrior.*

The attendants can lift him high on their shoulders and parade around the circle to the sound of applause and cheers.

A great feast should follow and the young man can feel free to order his attendants about or brag about his prowess on the battlefield.

When the ceremony is over, close the sacred space as normal, with thanks and an offering for the Old Ones as appropriate.

Attaining Manhood

Different events or stages of life are commonly recognised as conferring maturity. The physical signs of adulthood experienced during puberty appear quite early on in the teenage years but becoming an adult in every other sense of the word takes much longer. We need time to learn how to act responsibly, how to communicate effectively, how to live with respect for others, how to love and how to move on and make progress in our lives. When we have learned these lessons, often through heart-break, disappointment or lack of success, we arrive at a time and place when we start to feel and act like an adult instead of a youth.

Manhood and maturity encompass a variety of responsibilities and they are often taken very seriously. Taking on the role of being Mr Responsible or Mr Reliable to become the provider, hunter and protector, can often cause men to become very solemn and to put aside their spontaneity and laughter. Men are encouraged to take on these roles and states of mind by women, by other men and by the dreaded world of advertising and celebrity.

For men, recognising they have matured and reached that status of MAN comes with no awards or recognition from society or peers, the phase of knowing one has matured to manhood passes without being marked in any way. Whether it is a single event – having your first real lover – or a series of smaller occurrences that triggers off the awareness of reaching maturity, from the research I've done it seems that men, especially pagan men, would have greatly valued some way of marking the attainment of manhood.

Being a man should not be a burden, it does not have to mean you are always serious and lacking in humour, it does not mean you must always be the provider or defender, solely responsible for looking after the home and family. Being a man can mean enjoying your masculinity, taking control of your life and making sure you are happy with it. Sometimes this means you take on the role of the trickster god, rather than wise Greybeard – and what of that? Men are allowed to have fun, to take a break from the serious business of bringing in the money and putting food on the table. Isn't it time to acknowledge that men are not oppressed or bound by constraints and can express all emotions freely, even if they go against the commercial image of what men should be? Take charge of your masculinity and honour your manhood.

Guided Journey for Men

Before carrying out this journey, read through it and then ponder for a while on the benefits and drawbacks of being a man and make notes on what it means to you. Which god images do you identify with? Do you conform to any male stereotypes or are you unique? Does being a man limit or enhance you in any way?

Follow the usual procedures for starting a journey with a circle, invocations and preferably a fast-beat shamanic drumming tape to play during the journey or a live drummer if you are working in a group.

Rest, relax and guide yourself into trance. Start at your place of power and refrain from calling on your guide for assistance, if they are already present, ask them to leave you alone for this journey.

Walk away from your place of power in any direction you are drawn to – high hills, the depths of a cave or a bridge over a river. As you walk, take a mental note of what your surroundings are like, is it night or day? Is it warm or cold, can you hear birds or the rush of wind? Do you have to step over or move things out of your path? Think about what being a man means to you right now. Have you any roles or responsibilities that you feel apply to you as a man? How does being a man tie you down or free you up?

Keep walking and let yourself be drawn now to a large open space with a cliff along one side. See a massive, dark wooden door set into the side of the cliff and near this is an old, old man. The man gestures for you to enter the doorway, but what is it that you want to do?

The door leads to the underworld, the domain of the dark god, the one who is the hunter, the one who holds the secrets of the dark side of manhood. Go through this door if you want to meet with the dark god, he can answer questions and impart knowledge and wisdom and he can help with decision making or tell you how to bear the responsibilities of manhood.

A second door is also cut into the rock, this one made of shining metal. This door leads to the Upperworld, where you can meet with the green man. The green man is always depicted with a wide smile and leaves coming forth from his mouth – see these leaves as laughter and joy. The green man holds the secrets of being true to oneself; he holds dear joy, love, life and humour. He can tell you how to leave the seriousness and concerns behind you and get a lighter perspective on what manhood is all about. The green man can shine a torch at the light-hearted aspects of being a man.

The doors are slightly ajar, there is no way of knowing what lies inside. If you want to go through the doors and find out those secrets, go ahead. If you would rather sit in the sun and relax, if you would rather continue walking and thinking, then do that instead. The wisdom keeper, the old man, will only light the way. It is for you to decide if you want to walk the path.

You can enter either, neither or both of the doors. Meet with the dual aspects of male divinity to understand better how to live your life as a man, fully integrating all that it entails.

When you are done with this journey and have your answers from the gods, offer some token of respect in return for the wisdom, knowledge and insights you have received.

Travel back to your place of power, seeing if the path has changed or become any clearer to you. Any changes on the path are a sign that you have learned something or have progressed but only you will know what that may be. After giving thanks and returning the here and now, you should ideally spend some time considering the knowledge or insights you have gained from your journey.

Write down all your thoughts on the subject and then compare these notes to those you made earlier. What differences are there? Is there anything obvious you can do to integrate all of the aspects of manhood into your life more fully?

Close the circle as normal, giving thanks to the goddess, the god and the elements. Take action and make room in your life for expressing your masculinity in all its guises.

Fatherhood

Becoming a parent adds a new dimension to life and provides us with an ideal opportunity to prove how good we are at dealing with stress. Parenthood is not easy for anyone – society sees women as more inclined to be good at it than men only because their upbringing tends to push them towards it from an early age – but men are sensitive too and the birth of a child brings out that part of their nature.

Children are not just a responsibility or burden – they are damn good fun too. Playing with babies and children is rarely viewed as a good expression of manhood, but if men only ever take on the role of the stern, disciplinary parent, it can cut them off from their children. A doting father is a great asset to growing children who need to have a lot of laughter to help heal grazed knees. Men can often be more literal than women and this is valuable in communicating with very young children who are still piecing together their view of the world. Any small child will tell you instantly that daddies give the best piggy back rides and teenagers always appreciate Dad's wallet and taxi-service, even if they may not appreciate the rules that all parents, both mums and dads, are there to impose.

A good male role model is a boon to children and teenagers. In conventional partnerships, women appreciate the support they receive from men throughout pregnancy, birth and beyond. Fatherhood provides many opportunities to enjoy the simple things in life and any man who takes time to be actively involved in his children's upbringing will be grateful that he did so.

The Motherhood ritual given in chapter eight can be adapted with ease to honour your role as a father or a new ritual can be created for the occasion. Nor should men's feelings over a miscarriage be ignored or negated in favour of the grieving mother, it affects men deeply too and they are often forgotten about as everyone rallies round the woman with sympathy. The same or an adapted ritual as that given for women can be used for any man who wants to acknowledge and honour the loss of his unborn child.

Becoming an Elder

What do we conjure up in our minds when we think of mature or older men? The phrase 'old man' does not do much to honour everything that man has been in the past and continues to be in his mature years. Just as women can celebrate the end of their fertility and the coming of old age, so men can accept and honour the coming of their own wise years.

One of the most useful aspects of becoming an elder is being able to share the wisdom gained through a lifetime of experience. Encouraging others to learn, teaching traditional skills and techniques and the passing on of knowledge are very valuable yet highly underrated in our society. To recognise our worth as teachers and mentors is to bring an increase of self-esteem and self-worth and it brings benefits to our students too.

In the witchy community, young people tend to look upon elders as gurus or mentors who have been around forever and therefore they must know everything! Of course this is not the case, but from the newcomer's point of view, it can often come close. While being careful not to take advantage of the situation, an elder is able to smooth the path ahead for young people starting out on their journey of self-discovery. This does not mean an elder has all the answers but it can be of enormous benefit when a little bit of male logic is applied to difficult questions and comes out as words of wisdom, comfort or interest.

Being an elder can be a time of reflection or action, depending on the person but it certainly does not have to be boring. A man in his mature years can be every bit as fun-loving and open to new experience as a twenty-year old and there is no reason why he cannot continue to take part in all of the activities of that young age for as long good health allows. Mature men tend to be viewed as teachers, mentors and wisdom keepers. This is a high status and men can be proud to have it conferred on them.

Celebrating the Wiseman

The Wise Man is viewed as an old and solitary man; he is the hermit of the tarot cards to whom visitors come seeking answers to the problems of life. The wisdom keeper is a source we can tap into at any point in our lives but especially as we reach the stage when we pass from being fixated with virility and physical prowess and progress to the phase of accepting our wisdom and experiences as having worth and value to others.

To carry out a ritual in honour of the inner wisdom keeper, spend at least one full month thinking about what knowledge or experiences you have had that others might truly benefit from learning. Think also of a younger person with whom you would like to share this information – your own child, work colleagues, fellow Wiccans or a friend. Try and think of how you can present this information to them, it might be as a series of practical lessons in energy work or as a poetic text describing the cycles of the old gods. If you are new to the craft you will have still have some other skill you could pass down. Write it down on paper and curl it into a scroll to place on the altar as a token of your gift of wisdom. The elder should have the lines on his face enhanced with face-paints and is covered with a green cloth at the start of the ritual.

Create a sacred space and cast the circle with supportive friends and the younger person present, though not in the circle to begin with. Invoke the elements and call on the goddess and the horned god to lend their energies to the ritual. One man should act as the priest and the young person is referred to as neophyte.

The priest should begin by reading the following or something else appropriate to the man being recognised as elder.

Priest: *Horned God, Wisdom Keeper, Old Greybeard.*
Lover, brother, warrior, friend.
Seasons have passed from spring to summer,
Now autumn brings the winter near.
Teach us the dreams we can make real,
Bless us with insight to see things clearly.
Give us the wisdom we need to heal
As Old Greybeard lives with wisdom,
So let our new Elder possess these gifts.
Who comes here as an Elder? What is your name?'

Elder: *I am* (name) *and I am* (age) *years old. I have passed from youth to maturity and now I come here to claim my status as Elder and Wisdom Keeper.*

Priest: *Have you learned the secrets of the Gods?*

Elder: *I have learned the secrets of the God within myself.*

Priest: *Have you lived your life fully and loved well and faced up to your fears?*

Elder: *I have lived and loved and I have faced my fears.*

Priest: *Show me the signs of your wisdom.*

Elder: (takes off the cloth to reveal his face) *I bear the signs of wisdom on my face.*

Priest: *Then you are charged with the task of using your wisdom wisely. Have you chosen a neophyte to receive your gifts?*

Elder: *I call forward* (name) *to receive my gifts of wisdom.*

Neophyte: (Elder hands over the scroll) *I offer my thanks to you and accept the gift you pass onto me.*

Elder: *I am the Wisdom Keeper and my gift to you is… Will you use it wisely?*

Neophyte: *I will use the gifts wisely as you have instructed me.*

Priest: (Name), *we see that you are wise enough to share your secrets and pass on your skills. We grant you the status of Elder and Wisdom Keeper.*

Elder: *I accept my status as Elder and Wisdom Keeper. Blessed be.*

All: *Blessed be, Elder* (name).

The blessing of cakes and wine can now take place and the ritual closed to allow feasting and conversation to begin.

There is a responsibility with this ritual to follow it up by actually passing on and sharing your knowledge or skills, it is a promise in the presence of the Old Ones and your friends and the commitment should be carried out.

The God Within

The horned god is the archetype that most pagan and wiccan men associate with but the god has a multitude of dimensions that can be tapped into. From Loki and the other trickster gods we have a streak of unruly havoc or mischief making; Pan offers men an image of seduction and playfulness; he is wild, randy, bi-sexual and musical; Odin represents wisdom, courage and strength; the god Lugh is intelligent and benevolent; Bran gives men an image of poetic compassion combined with power.

Men have a wide choice of mythical gods to associate with and it is a great shame that so many men are stuck in the roles that gender stereotyping slots them into. A man who is completely at ease with himself is able to show his sensitive side as well as his brave or macho side.

To integrate fully all the brilliance of men, a journey is offered here as a template to base your own journey on. Prepare as normal with a sacred space and relaxation then start your journey in your place of power, the inner temple.

Ask for the god to visit you in the aspect or archetype you most need to bring into your life. Watch the direction the god comes from and take note of his appearance – is he the hunter, the green man, old or young?

Greet the god and ask if you can talk together for a time. Explain that you want to become fully integrated with all the traits of manhood and ask for help in recognising what they are. Find out if you have too much of one and not enough of another. Ask how you can deal with any imbalance in a practical sense.

Enquire about any burning issues you have to deal with and having got this out of the way, ask if the god will tell you the secrets of being empowered and fully alive as a man. Spend as long as you need posing questions or gaining insight into manhood and when you are finished talking with this aspect of the god, ask to see others and find out what they have to offer you.

When you have received the answers you need, see if Herne the Hunter will come to you. Ask him to show you the secrets of the forest, walk and talk together, hunt together through the woods and across the moors, be a part of the wild hunt and accept that every part of being a man is yours to keep forever.

Come to rest when the talking and the hunting are over and return to your place of power. State loudly an affirmation on this theme.

'I am the God made man, I am strong, I am wise, I am all that man can be and I accept the gifts of manhood.'

Write up your journey experience to help you remember any useful thoughts and decisions. Give thanks to the god in all his glorious aspects and bring yourself slowly back to the here and now. Close down your sacred space in the usual manner and be proud to take your place in the world as an embodiment of the god.

CHAPTER 8

Power Animals

For thousands of years animals have played a large part in our lives from our domesticated kitty who plays at being our comforter when she's not busy hunting to the horse who until recently carried us into battle and still in some areas draws our plough through the fields. Hunting wild beasts for food and leather, rearing captive animals for food, transportation, companionship and more – we have long associations with many animal species. Our shamans and priests dressed in animal skins in their rituals to bring that animal's strength, power and abilities into their magic to make it more powerful. Rural traditions involving animals for sympathetic magic have been handed down through the generations and expressions like '*Hair of the dog that bit you*' used to have a very literal meaning – a bite wound would be bandaged with a few hairs of the offending dog in the belief that this would make the wound heal more quickly.

Animals offer strength, support, guidance and inspiration. From tiny ants to giant elephants, every creature on earth has its purpose and animals have been revered and honoured by native people from all over the world. No matter how small and seemingly insignificant they may be, all living creatures can help us understand our nature, solve problems, offer reassurance and lead us further along our path of spiritual enlightenment. Through studying the natural environment, behaviour and life style of a particular animal as well as interacting with our animal guides in the other realms, we come to know the creature and recognise its various traits.

There is often some confusion about whether we should call these animal guides *power animals* or *totem animals* and if there is really any difference between the two. The word totem refers to a natural object or animal which has spiritual significance for those who use it; a totem animal can therefore be described as an animal with spiritual significance to the individual, family or tribe. The word *power* means the inherent ability and authority of an individual to act; in this sense a power animal can lend us the ability and authority to act in a certain way. Power animals are seen as more intrinsic to an individual than a totem animal; they represent the inner power and abilities of a person where a totem animal can be seen as one that is meaningful to that person for some other reason. There have been times when I've been discussing this subject with people and been told off for saying one word when they themselves use the other but I've found that if I use the term animal guide, people understand what I mean by that without pressing their own term upon me. For me, the term animal guide means an animal with whom I have a relationship in the other realms for guidance, companionship and insights.

When we hear the phrase *totem animal* or *power animal* the first images that come to mind are animals like the wolf, eagle, bear or some other animal of similar significance and strength. If you really feel that you're being drawn to a particular animal with these overt attributes of physical prowess, it could certainly be true that it is your animal guide. However, I have spoken with people in the past who have no experience of these animals in either the real world or in the world beyond worlds – in other words, because they are admire or feel a pull towards that animal they have assumed (or desperately wish) that say, a giant wolf with snow-white fur is their personal animal spirit without once going through a single journey or quest to find out if that is actually the case.

Perhaps your animal guide is a wolf but what if you go on a trance journey and find out that your animal guide is a worm, a mouse or a cow? Laugh if you will, and people do, but why should a bear, wolf, stag or eagle have any more significance than a worm? A bear is strong, full of protective spirit, a hunter and yet a gentle parent and certainly bear has much to teach us. A worm, however, turns and churns the very earth we live on and rely on. Without worms, our compost would be lifeless and our crops would begin to fail – they may be tiny but the worm nourishes us, turns old matter into a new and life enriching soil for growth and sustenance. Worms are the ultimate recyclers – from the worm, we learn that in giving up those emotions which are not beneficial, jealousy, anger, bitterness or hatred, we can let it go, bury it, recycle it and turn it into something brighter and more giving and loving. We turn anger into understanding, jealously into acceptance and hatred into love. What more powerful lesson could we learn from our animal guide?

Animals guides are not set in stone either and they can change – you don't necessarily have the same animal guide for your entire life. You might find that you've spent a few years building up a relationship with horse only to find out that horse is leaving you in the care of a new creature, the crow. So now you have to say farewell and thank you to horse for its lessons and gifts and learn about crow energy and how that relates to your life. Crow might only be with you for a few months or he could stay with you for the rest of your life. Perhaps crow has been in the background for a while, unseen, hiding and waiting until you needed his energy.

Something like this happened with my own animal guide. Ever since I was a very small child I have been mad about horses and although I no longer ride, I used to at every opportunity and would arrive at my local stables as early as possible just so that I could be near the horses for as long as I could. My earliest dream recollection, aged around five, was about horses and they have been a regular feature of my dreams ever since. When I first started to do trance and journey work many years ago, the animal guide who came to me was a hulking great big stag who bellowed at me with a deep *hhhrrrnn* like call. Stag disappeared for a few years, during which time I had other animal guides but stag returned to me later on and is still there for me now when I need him. All of this time, however, I was still seeing horses at significant times and in my dreams so I wanted to get to the bottom of this and went through a deep journey to investigate.

Deep in the forest of my sacred inner space, I asked my guide, a cranky old chap with cantankerous tendencies, to help me find out what horses mean for me. He didn't say a word, instead he turned his back on me and, leaning heavily on his staff, he walked off. I duly followed and was led away from the sacred space to an open valley where at the bottom of a stream was a herd of white horses. My guide hobbled away and left me there with these horses so I introduced myself to them. The horses took very little notice of me, harrumphing and stomping hooves, they just continued to munch the grass and bask in the sunshine.

However, I had been spotted by one horse who eventually came over to me and we spoke about why I had been seeing horses at regular intervals since my earliest memories. I was told that Horse is my life-totem and other creatures who come to me are my animal guides for a specific purpose, coming into my life as and when I need them. Horses will always be there for me, I couldn't shake them off if I wanted to, while other animals are more transient. Not only this, I was given very clear and precise information about what different coloured horses mean when I see them in the real world or in dreams and visions. Piebalds, skewbalds, greys, chestnut, black horses, bays and roans all have different meanings and that can change slightly if they are galloping towards me, blocking my way, being ridden or grazing when I encounter them. I was told that horses don't actually live in a herd – they call it a tribe – and I was introduced to several unicorns, winged horses and winged unicorns. The mythical horses were not all white and light and lovely as we have been led to believe – every animal has a dark side just as we have our own darkness within.

After this very specific information on the meanings of horses and their kin (and it's very personal to me so won't be disclosed here), I was invited to ride on the back of a winged unicorn. Wind in my hair, my fingers wrapped in his mane, soaring above the trees and away from the valley of the horses and back to my sacred space in the forest where my guide was waiting for me with a sulky look in his eyes. 'Never give me a lift back, little buggers,' he said. I laughed and gradually came back to the here-and-now, making lots of notes in my book of shadows.

So your animal guide could be just one animal for all time or it might change, depending on your circumstances and what advice or healing or strength you need to get through a particular situation.

Making the Connection

So how do we find our animal guides to communicate with and learn from them? The simple yet cryptic answer is that *they* find *you.* Your animal guide will start appearing to you, seemingly at random, on pictures, postcards, billboard posters or in films and documentaries. Your power animal might come to you in your dreams or while out walking you might find a raven's feather, smell the musky scent of a fox or hear an owl hooting unexpectedly. If this sounds familiar or if there is an animal you have always felt drawn to, this is a clue that it could be your animal guide but as we have seen, it is important to find out for certain and not just to assume. The surest way of doing this is through the deep trance journeys like the ones we have carried out to meet with our guide, the anima and animus and with the god and goddess.

Our shaman ancestors were adept at these deep journeys and today there are still shamans who are skilled enough to bring forward an animal guide not only for themselves but on behalf of another person and then to make a psychic link between them. Being able to journey yourself to the other realms and meet your guides is a powerful additional to your witchy tool kit. By going through these journeys and quests, we become more empowered as witches and healers and explore our inner selves, our deepest, secret souls. In discovering our animal guide and connecting with it, we gain another aspect of the psyche that expands our spiritual awareness and opens us to new insights and experiences.

Journey Time

Set aside some time and create a sacred space or circle in which you can sit comfortably and without interruption. Still your thoughts and visualise the space being surrounded by a silver or white glowing light, cast your circle and invoke the Old Ones, the elements, Lord and Lady, spirit of your ancestors and spirit of the place.

Relax deeply, use the rainbow countdown and open your chakras and spend a while visualising your sacred space, exactly as you have done before. See it clearly, feel yourself truly there, away from this world in another realm.

Ask for your guide to come to you and when s/he appears, explain that you are ready to meet your animal guide. Clear your mind of all images and preconceptions of what you think that animal will be. Ask your guide to set up a meeting with your animal. He might create a mist in your sacred space for your animal to appear or he could lead you to the animal or bird or water creature. Be aware of your surroundings and any pathways or journeys you take to get there – is it daytime, early morning or night? What season are you in and what is the weather like? As you wait to meet your animal guide do you hear any noises of birds, rustlings in the leaves, the sound of a bubbling stream or wind rushing on a high cliff top? All of these might be significant when you find out what animal is going to be working with you.

When you meet this animal guide, be respectful and thankful. Take plenty of time to explore your thoughts with this creature, share your dreams and ask your questions and offer something in return. Find out why this animal in particular has shown itself to you – does it have information for you? Does it have a particular power you can take with you? Will this animal stay with you, does it have a name you can call it? Are you being shown the animal in its natural environment? How is its message relevant to your current circumstances? Can it help you with any indecision or guide you through a difficult experience? Animals often appear to us exactly when we need them the most and the insights they give can be a revelation.

Take all the time you need and when you are ready to leave take note of any instructions, advice, wisdom or gifts. Give thanks, say farewell and return to your sacred space. Gradually, keeping with you all that you have discovered, return to the here and the now and the everyday reality.

Slowly rise up, clap your hands, have something to eat and drink to ground yourself and be fully aware of your surroundings again. Write down in as much detail as you can everything that has happened and what was said or done in your journey.

Before you close your circle, sit in silence and ask that all the information and insight you have gained will stay with you and take hold in your subconscious mind.

Give thanks to the god and goddess, the spirits of your home and the elements in their quarters. Offer up some small token to the spirits of nature in recognition of their help and advice. This might mean donating to an animal charity or making sure you replenish the nuts in your garden bird-feeder. Giving something back and making an offering shows our respect and honours our guides and the Old

Ones, the give-away is an important step that our ancestors have been doing for centuries. It's well known that Native Americans make regular offerings, often of tobacco, to their gods, their guides, the earth and their ancestors. Only a couple of generations ago here in Britain, we used to leave out bread or biscuits and a little milk or whisky as an offering to the Little People – our spirits of the land – to please them and curry favour. A tradition worth sticking to, I believe, especially when our spirit guides, animal, human or otherwise, have been so ready to speak with us and guide us.

Animal Meanings

Regularly meeting your new-found animal guide is important, for without frequent contact with our companions we lose touch and have to work at redeveloping any closeness we used to have. Visit often and take long walks in silence with your animal guide, sit and talk, swim and play together, fly in the skies or rest in its lair – take time to develop a solid affinity.

Animal guides often show up in the real world too, often at significant turning points in our lives. When I see a roan pony I know that it means – well, sometimes it just means I've walked past a field where a roan pony is grazing. Sometimes, however, if I'm driving and thinking about something important or worrying or turning a decision over and over in my mind, I happen to catch a glance of that horse at just the right moment then it can make me to stop and think – is this a sign? Is this important? Often, the answer will be there instantly – yes, this is relevant to what I was thinking about, but sometimes I will need to work through it a little or visit my animal guide in a trance to find out and ask deeper, more succinct questions.

Seeing our animal guides in the physical world isn't always a sign of something deep and meaningful, it might be purely coincidental but it's always worth investigating.

It is also helpful to pay attention to the real animals around us. Messages don't always come in the form of a dream or vision or journey and it won't always be our animal guide who delivers that message – seeing a frog unexpectedly when you're going through a period of change might have some significance for you even if frog is not one of your known animal guides. Look out for animals, birds, fish, newts, spiders and insects next time you're outdoors and see how many different types of creature you spot – look up their meanings and traits and learn about them and how it could relate to your life. If you find nothing of relevance, you still have something valuable, you've learned a little more about the natural we live in and a new appreciation of that animal and how it lives.

Learning about animal guides doesn't have to be based on books or teachings about shamanic power animals or spirit animal totems, it comes from observing and learning about real animals and their natural behaviours and environments. If you have found out that you do have an animal guide, find out what you can about its world, habits, family groups and survival traits so that you can really understand and grasp the significance of it in your own life.

Mammals

Badger – a quick and sometimes aggressive animal, badger fights to protect what he owns. Elusive and cautious, badgers live in family groups in massive underground tunnel systems with separate toilet and sleeping areas. Badgers sets are passed on to successive generations with continual expansions over several decades and longer. Badger energy helps you to defend and stand up for yourself and shows you how to get to the core, or root, of a problem.

Bear – often seen as a warrior or protector, bear is connected to the spirit realms through the constellation of Ursur Major, the great bear. Bear is an animal who can connect us to our spirituality and with the other realms – bear hunts just as well over water or land and is seen as strong and fierce. Tap into bear energy if you need to defend yourself. The long hibernation of a bear within a cave symbolises our need to withdraw from our environment and reflect and meditate on our long-term goals.

Deer – while they can be aggressive in their rut, deer are normally very gentle creatures, remaining in the shadows of deep woodland. Deer spend most of the time in single sex groups, coming together only for the yearly rutting season. A stag's antlers start to grow in the early summer and are fully grown in the autumn. Antlers are normally shed before or around Imbolc, when the does are preparing to give birth to their young and still today people dress in deer antlers for rituals and mummers plays. The deer can represent strength and independence too and the stag is associatėd with Herne the hunter and Cernunnos. Deer brings us grace, majesty and a sense of serenity and is also associated with fertility rites.

Fox – Foxes live in family groups and are scavengers as well as hunters. The ability of fox to be cunning in his decisions and keenly observant of other creatures around him while remaining unseen himself means that fox has discretion and patience, the ability to watch and assess a situation wisely before acting. If fox comes into your life, think about displaying more patience.

Horse – The horse is a herd animal and so lends energy to all relationships. Horse is also seen as a messenger or carrier and can help with communication. Their gentle nature combines with great strength and endurance and can indicate the need for perseverance, determination and strength of character. Horses can represent inner strength, physical strength and the need to make progress and travel onwards. Horse creates solid relationships and friendships and tells us to be supportive of others. Horses are often seen as a creature who helps us to move forwards and onwards.

Lion – Almost universally, lions are seen as strong, fiery and majestic beasts. Their ability to recover quickly after sudden exertion makes lion a good ally for healing of any kind. However, as a member of the cat family, lions are actually pretty lazy, sleeping for up to twenty hours a day and not quite the stunningly good hunters they would like to be. The power and leadership qualities of lion can help you with issues of confidence and assertiveness while reassuring us that life doesn't have to be that hard and it's okay to sit back and relax.

Mouse – Tiny mouse is prey for many animals and so pays close attention to his surroundings, constantly on the lookout for predators and ready to dart away at the slightest hint of movement. The wood mouse can shed the end of its tail when caught and mice can jump long distances to get out of trouble. If mouse comes to you, not everything may be as it seems, watch out for the hidden agendas of others. Mouse warns us to examine the small, seemingly insignificant details, of our problems while keeping one eye on the bigger picture and tells us that sometimes we must let go of one thing to gain another.

Squirrel – The hordes of nuts a squirrel collects and buries are indicative of clever foresight and planning. Squirrels are busy and active creatures, alert to possibilities and keenly protective. Squirrels can be nosey and curious and scamper quickly through the trees or they can be patient, still and watchful. Squirrel teaches good organisation skills and tells us to make good use of our time as well as bringing a sense of energetic playfulness.

Weasel – Adaptable weasel can survive in almost any environment from sand dunes and grasslands to woodlands and mountains. They are active both night and day and prey on small rodents like mice or voles and will eat eggs and birds when they can. There's a lot of folklore and superstition regarding weasels – you can never catch a weasel asleep, it's bad luck for a weasel to cross your path, especially if he's wearing his winter-white coat, and a squeaking weasel near your house is an omen of death. Weasel has been seen for a long time as playful and cunning but also as sly, not quite trustworthy and having an ability to put people on edge. Weasel is a warning but this isn't a bad thing – forewarned is forearmed. Weasel also offers adaptability and resourcefulness.

Wolf – often viewed as a dangerous predator, wolf is a great protector of family and home and incredibly loyal and faithful. Wolf families have defined relationships, with the alpha male in position of leader. We have seen the wolf in Europe as having a bad reputation as hunters and the expression of a sheep in wolf's clothing refers to someone who is not all they seem to be and who turns out to be deceitful and nasty. In Native American traditions though, the wolf is seen as a teacher and guide and if wolf appears to you, you should be alert as some new learning or knowledge is on its way to you.

Birds

Corvids – Crows, ravens, rooks and jays are all corvids. There are over 120 species and most of them form life-time pairings. They are very clever birds, dropping nuts on roads so that passing cars will crush them open and they manage to work out the most elaborate of mazes and puzzles. Crows and ravens are both seen as harbingers of doom and death and raven especially is associated with the underworld. The Norse god Odin has two ravens, Hugin and Munin, who act as his messengers and spies. A collection of crows is called a murder while rooks gather in a parliament. So under the guidance of these birds we can be resourceful, clever and astute – they see things we may not see and warn us of impending danger.

Eagle – soaring high and endowed with crystal clear vision, eagle tells you to reach for your dreams and goals with determination and a clear plan. Eagle has strong associations with Native American culture and is a powerful bird with excellent vision. View the goals from outside the box and keep yourself open to all possibilities.

Magpie – another member of the corvid family, magpies have a wealth of folkore all of their own. Instantly recognisable with their black and white feathers, they are widely distributed across the country, with the exception of the Scottish highlands. The old rhyme goes: one for sorrow, two for mirth, three for a funeral, four for a birth, five for silver, six for gold, seven for a secret never to be told: there are several versions of the rhyme, one of which of states that it's one for sorrow, two for joy, three for a girl and four for a boy. Single magpies are an omen of bad times ahead so if you see only one, assume that another is nearby or bad luck is on its way. Many people, not only witches, make a point of saying hello to magpies and if you see a solitary magpie you should say *'Good morning Mister Magpie, how's your beautiful wife?'*

Owl – the only bird that flies in total silence, owl is a night hunter and sees things others cannot. Owls are associated with the Cailleach and the cycle of death and rebirth. The celtic flower maiden, Blodeuwedd, wife of Lleu Llaw Gyffes, is turned into an owl when she betrays him and she forever remains on the threshold of this world and the next, unable to live fully in either. The owl gives us the secrets of the underworld, the gift of hidden knowledge and insight and is a reminder that in death we are reborn.

Robin – Robin is the bird who tried to pull thorns from the crown Jesus wore at the crucifixion, staining his chest bright red. It's still considered very bad luck to kill a robin – in fact it is illegal to kill a robin, take its eggs or disturb its nest. Males and females both have the red-breast but not the young; they are violently territorial birds and will fight to the death all year round to defend their territory. Robin's message as a guide is of loyalty, standing up for ourselves and what we have worked hard to achieve and to also stand up for others and what we believe is the right thing to do.

Swan – representing loyalty in love, truth, purity and integrity. Swans mate for life and are fierce protectors of their nests and their young. Fairy tales about swans have them transforming in human shape or vice versa and living in different kingdoms or worlds for long periods before returning and transforming back into human form, sometimes with one arm still as a wing. The romantic image of two swans with their wings and necks positioned like a floating heart is quite endearing but from the folklore about swans, we see they have a deeper meaning than just enduring love. Swans give us a way to see both sides of a story and help us to cope with living far apart from our kin.

Other Creatures

Frog and Toad – With their amphibious adaptability both frog and toad lend you the courage to take the plunge, to dive into new situations or relationships and strive for change. Frogs used to be rubbed over warts to make them disappear and were sometimes associated with witches who were rumoured to keep them as their familiars. Medicines and charms have been made using dried frogs and toads and hallucinogenic drugs made from their skins, something akin to the witches flying ointment. They are connected to both water and earth and can be seen as a traveller or guide from one reality to another and as a powerful guide for deep journey work.

Lizard – most lizards have live young in cold climates and lay eggs in warmer climates, they hibernate during the winter and can swim underwater to avoid predators. They can also shed their tails to escape capture and they are cold-blooded, warming themselves by basking on logs and trees in the sun.

Old folklore of England says that a lizard is bad luck for a bride though if it runs over a woman's hand, she will be a good craftswoman. However, lizards can only shed their tails once, a warning to us that when we have a big decision to make, we must make sure it's the right decision as the consequences are long-lasting.

Snake – Venomous snakes use their poison to hunt and kill and rarely for defence while non-venomous snakes kill by suffocation or swallowing live prey. Grass snakes play dead when cornered and lay eggs while Adders have live young. With its patient waiting, silent movement and the ability to shed its skin, snake teaches us about rebirth and helps us to live through traumatic times with the knowledge that as one chapter in our lives comes to an end, all things live on and a new stage can begin. Snake shows us that sometimes we must just wait, watch and be alert for opportunity.

Mythical Animals

I won't go into the hundreds of thousands of mythical creatures like the kelpie, fairies, gorgons, krakens, selkies or the phoenix and nor will I delve into the realms of paranormal or supernatural with vampires, werewolves, the Chupacabra, or the mothman because there are just too many, instead we shall focus on just a few that seem to be most popular!

Dragon – Fiery beasts with a love of gold, old castles and mountain ranges, dragons have great power and fiery breath to fend off enemies and protect sacred treasures. Dragon advises you that your greatest treasure – your soul – may have been neglected. Take time to look after yourself and recuperate from whatever difficulties you have experienced. Dragon energy can be called in to protect the home while you are away or stand guard at your circle or to offer strength, courage and determination. Dragons are associated with fire, of course, and you may want to call on dragon energy for powerful protection rituals or spells that use the element of fire.

Gryphon – With the head and wings of an eagle and the body and tail of a lion, the Gryphon has the attributes of both these animals. The mystical Gryphon mates for life and like dragon, he loves treasure and gold and is equally happy on land or in the air. Gryphon is concerned with protection, faithfulness and loyalty and is supposed to turn away anyone who is greedy, needy and dishonest. The Gryphon protects the home and family and can be invoked when performing love-spells for that much sought-after long-term relationship.

Mermaid – Sea or river dwelling, mermaids are traditionally female with long hair which they comb with spiny shells while basking on rocks in the open sea, calling lusty sailors to their aid. Upon reaching the mermaid, our hapless sailor is dragged down into the ocean's depths, never to be seen again. Occasionally, she turns him into a merman and marries him. The mermaid can be viewed as the archetypal dark feminine, the beautiful woman who has a hidden side and shows us what lies beyond death. A spirit of water, mermaids can offer a journey to meet with your deeper soul, the subconscious, to bring balance to your emotions.

Unicorn – Not just a horse with a horn, the unicorn is blessed with magical powers and is normally pictured drinking from a stream in a beautiful green valley or clearing with a rainbow or waterfall in the background. Normally pure white and full of grace, a typical unicorn can only be caught or ridden by a virgin maiden and represents purity, truth and honesty. To harm or kill a unicorn is an unforgivable crime in the legends and fairy tales and only a pure soul can ride one. Living with honesty, following your intuition and living according to your values and morals is unicorn's message.

CHAPTER 9

Healing

Healing within witchcraft can take the form of spells, candle magic, poppets, rituals, prayers, hands-on healing, herbs and crystals. Many witches and pagans go on courses to learn complementary therapies, some of which are discussed in more detail below than others. This is deliberate on my part as anything which physically acts on the body should be administered by somebody who has been trained to do that to avoid any possible mistakes or misdiagnoses where medicines are concerned and this is best left to professionals – even aromatherapy, as we will see, has to be done with care – while other therapies are safe to try yourself. Reiki and crystal healing are both such simple and safe therapies that I have provided a little more information about them and would thoroughly recommend these therapies to try out with your group or other willing volunteers. Although Reiki does have to be 'taught', it is inexpensive and very easy to learn. Crystal healing is instantly accessible and there are guide books to help you through the maze of different crystals.

Witches have been associated with healing for centuries and it's nice to be able to carry on the tradition even when we are not healers, nurses, vets or doctors. Not only are we trying to do some good in the world, we are hopefully making a real difference to somebody who needs it and it is also a way of giving-back and offering something of ourselves to others and to the Old Ones whose names we honour in our rites.

Healing rituals within the coven can be very powerful, especially if all coveners personally know the recipient, as every witch is working together with the same goal in mind at the same and with the aid of charms, candles, anointing oils, poppets, appropriate colours, using relevant god and goddess names and channelling energy in a cone of power. If possible, place a photograph of the person being healed on the altar, select crystals and oils or incenses that are in tune with healing their condition. Make sure you have permission of the person you are working healing for beforehand.

Poppets

Poppets are essentially a small cloth doll used to represent the person you are doing magic for. The poppet doesn't need to be elaborately hand-sewn and embroidered with gold threads and beads, it can just be two roughly human-shaped pieces of cloth sewn up with a little bit of wadding to pad it out a bit (my gran used to chop up old socks and tights as stuffing). Small buttons can be sewn on for eyes or you can sew a face on or draw it with fabric pens. Small healing crystals and little bundles of appropriate herbs can be placed inside the poppet and it can have some ribbon tied round the waist in your patient's favourite colour to make a psychic link or even put a small photograph of the person inside before you sew it up. This psychic link should be strengthened if the healing is to have any effect. If at all possible, all the materials, gems, etc for the poppet should be on your altar and the doll made up during a ritual inside the circle. Consecrate the doll and then link it in with the intended person.

Little cloth doll, we give you life. Little cloth doll, your name is Judy. Judy doll, open your eyes, we bring you to life, little cloth doll, we bring you healing and health.

Put the doll to your mouth and breathe over it, visualising Judy as you do. Now begin to raise energy in the circle by dancing and drumming. A two or three word chant such as

Judy, healthy, healing, happy

to go along with this and the burning of pink healing candles anointed with lavender oil or rosemary (or other herb) will all add to the energy. When you feel the power is starting to rise, the chant becomes faster, the dancing more energetic, the energy rises and when it peaks, use your wand to direct it down into the doll.

The doll can be kept safe on the altar if necessary but for preference, give the doll to Judy to keep with her at all times – the doll can lay beside her at night and live in her hand bag or on her work desk or wherever during the day so that the healing will be passed on to her. Alternatively, if you keep the poppet on your altar, you can do more healing work for your friend next time you have a circle or play at nursing the doll to pass on healing thoughts whenever you tend your altar.

Candles

Candle magic has been done to death in hundreds of books and pamphlets and workshops but there's a reason for that – it's effective, it's accessible, it doesn't require any complicated sigils or equipment and it's simple. That doesn't mean it's easy. To work well candle magic has to have a lot of focus and will power dedicated to it. Your intentions count.

Candles come in every shade of every colour so choose one that you think will be beneficial to your particular patient. A quick internet search or browse through the books and you can find out what colours might be appropriate; if in doubt, go with what appeals to you, what you are intuitively drawn towards. Pale pink candles are good for general healing, red for circulatory, kidney or heart problems, orange for mental and emotional healing, treating depression or stress, purple or indigo for glandular disorders and eye health, blue for the throat, mouth and ears, green for heart and lung conditions, and yellow is for digestive problems and is a good colour for nervous disorders.

To prepare a healing candle spell set up your circle and with everything consecrated, heat a small pin or the tip of your athame in the flame of an altar candle and use it to carve healing words and the name of the person along the length of the healing candle. Annoint it with a few drops of relevant essential oil in a carrier oil to make it go further, smoothing the oil into the candle from the centre to the tip and base. Roll the candle in healing herbs so they stick to the outside and then place the candle in a secure holder.

A photograph of the person on the altar will help, as will talking about them for a few minutes so that everybody involved can get a clear mental image that will aid with focus and intention. We have already seen how solar and lunar phases can be used to aid magic so this is worth bearing in mind too, remembering that a waning moon could be used to get rid of illness while the sun at its mid-day height and power might be harnessed for strength and vitality for the person you are healing.

When the ritual space is ready and the candle secured, light it and begin to channel energy into it, from the earth and sky, above and below, through your body, out through the palm centres and into the candle as it burns and glows. Visualise clearly, focus deeply on the person being whole, healthy, free of disease and completely happy. Think it, feel it, say it:

> *Mark, you are healthy, Mark, you are strong, Mark you are back to your old self again. Healthy and happy and healthy and free, as I do will, so mote it be!*

Keep every single word and thought focused on a healthy image of Mark and keep channelling that light energy while the candle burns down.

If it's not possible to let the candle burn down completely, there are two ways you can save it and repeat the healing magic another time. One way is to pierce the candle all the way through with a needle, or several needles if using a large candle, leaving the needle in place through the centre of the candle – as the candle burns down to the needle put it out and repeat the process the following day. However, if like me, you try to pierce the candle with a needle and only succeed in breaking the thing in two, you can tie a piece of thin sewing cotton round the candle at intervals instead with the same method of putting out the flame once it reaches that marker and repeat the next day.

Hands on Healing

Performing healing when the person being treated is actually present has deeper and more successful results than any distance healing is likely to have. If it's appropriate and the person you are healing is pagan or at least understands the basic premise of ritual and what you are doing, then you would be present for her, cast a circle around her, invoking the elements and the god and goddess and carry out the healing work within this sacred space. If that's not possible for whatever reason, then at the very least explain that you will create a peaceful atmosphere and set up a sacred space. Use low lighting, a few candles, have soft and luxurious drapes if you can – though if you are doing this in a hospital or hospice, you will just have to work with what you can get away with. Even having a potted plant or bunch of flowers at the bedside will be a help.

If your patient can, have her sit or lie down comfortably and position yourself so that you can move easily around her. Starting with a few minutes of deep relaxation while you open your chakras, talk your friend through a relaxing exercise and then start to tap in to the energy channels that run through your body and connect you to the higher powers of the universal life force. Feel it running through you, into your hands, filling you with a constant flow of power and healing, see it as a shining pastel-coloured light, pink or soft green or white, and breathe in deeply. Place your hands gently on the crown chakra of the recipient, see that brilliant healing light flowing to them, through you and into their crown to start the healing process. Keep that energy softly pulsing, pull it up from the earth, down from the stars, visualise it clearly.

Now take your hands slightly away from the patient's body and slowly run your hands up and down their aura and let yourself notice instinctively where the aura feels unsettled, shadow-like or filled with blockages. Pay attention to any areas your hands are drawn to, not doing anything for now, just being aware of it and remembering the sensation. You may need to scan the aura a few times to feel anything, especially as you start out – practice on a friend. Once your body and aura scan is done, bring that flow of energy back through your hands and direct it to the spots where you feel drawn to. Be guided by your intuition. Hold your hands above the body for as long as that flow is strong and specific and then gradually move to the other areas where you feel healing is needed or focus on each of the chakra points in turn. All the time, you should be sensing that continual pulse of healing from the universal energy source, the god and goddess, through your hands and being directed to your healing recipient. Focus clearly on the healing and picture your friend full of relaxing, beneficial healing, as healthy and well as they could possibly be.

A healing mantra or chant can be repeated while you do this or play a meditation cd in the background to create a completely relaxing experience. Combine this with a prayer to the Lord and Lady for healing and well-being.

> *I ask for this healing energy to give Kerry good health, fill her with vitality and energy, vibrant and wholesome. Great Goddess, let Kerry be filled with healing, with love and with light. I ask the elements of air, fire, water, earth and spirit to lend energy and*

healing, come through me and into Kerry for rejuvenation and good health. Let her be healed, let her be whole, as I do will, so mote it be.

Combine this healing energy with candle magic and crystals placed around the patient to increase the power behind it and if your friend is a witch or understands what you are doing, then you could raise energy for a cone of power and as it peaks, direct itsenergy to her.

Make sure that when you are finished, you place your hands once more on the crown chakra and also on the feet for grounding. Give thanks to the god and goddess, the elements and the healing energy.

Complementary Therapies

The majority of complementary therapies and medicines, sometimes referred to as 'alternative' therapies, are the intuitive or medical healing disciplines of our ancestors and it was not that long ago that current medical practice and medicines actually came to be accepted as the norm. Only a few generations ago, we all knew that lavender could be used for insomnia or we called comfrey knit-bone, due its bone healing properties and the hard poultice made from it that was used to make a cast around broken bones. It seems such a shame that this valuable knowledge has been largely lost to the general population who now turn to expensive synthetic medicines when not that long ago we had much more natural and usually just as effective ways of treating illness and disease.

Complementary therapies are a bit of a minefield but it's certainly worth investigating a few to see if any of these can be added to your repertoire of skills. After all, our witchy ancestors were the wise-men and women who people turned to for medicines and healing and it does feel really good when you are able to help, even in some small way, when somebody you care for is suffering. The few listed here are just the tip of the ice-berg – we haven't even got off ground here - and if you are drawn to any of them, there is a lot of research ahead of you to master them but it is nice to think that we can follow in the steps of our ancestors.

Massage and aromatherapy are widely used for relaxation, relief of muscular aches and pains and for sports injuries but can have a much deeper implication for healing. A fully qualified masseuse and/or aromatherapist will, like other healers, start with an initial consultation to take a full and detailed history of the patient's symptoms, physical, mental and emotional. This enables them to make an assessment of the patient and form a diagnosis and course of treatment based on a holistic view of their patient. Any essential oils used may have counter-indications that they will have to be aware of and there could be conditions that mean certain massage techniques need to be avoided so massage and aromatherapy isn't just a more complex form of comforting back-rub but has very detailed expertise behind it.

A masseuse will have a good working knowledge and understanding of anatomy and physiology and years of training and practical experience. Sports injury massage is another more detailed discipline which again takes years of study and training and has very good, proven results.

Medical herbalism encompasses a wide range of herbs and plants that are turned into poultices, creams, lotions, mouth-washes, topical treatments and oral medicines to treat physical and emotional symptoms and disorders. Medical herbalism takes several years of study at degree or post-graduate level and includes the diagnosis of illnesses and disease followed by treatment with carefully prepared herbs, a full background or patient history, several consultations and follow up appointments. Medical herbalists are strictly governed and must be accredited and registered in order to practice and while we may be able to make our own lavender bath salts for relaxation and to ease muscular aches and pains, great care must be taken to ensure that you know exactly what herbs to use and, more importantly, when not to use them. As an example of this, St John's Wort (hypericum) can be used to treat depression but may interact adversely with medications including contraception, migraine relief (sumatriptan) blood thinning agents (warfarin), immunosuppressant and heart medications such as digoxin. A qualified medical herbalist will take a full medical and life-style history to get a complete picture of the patient's symptoms, diagnose any disease or illness and decide which herbal remedy or combination of remedies can be used to treat the person holistically.

Chiropractic care has a particular focus on the spine and the musculo-skeletal system and assumes that vertebral subluxations or spinal dysfunction can cause interference and disease in the bodily system as a whole and correction, or adjustment, of these sublulxations will bring symptomatic relief and improve the overall health and wellness of the body.

D.D. Palmer was the pioneer of chiropractic in the 1890s and it was seen as quite controversial as he had no conventional medical training. Even so, the techniques he developed gradually became an accepted way of treating a wide range of disorders, especially in America. McTimoney Chiropractic was developed by John McTimoney over fifty years ago and is only taught at the McTimoney Chiropractic College near Oxford. The McTimoney approach, like other therapies, takes a whole-body, holistic view of the healing process, based around the adjustment of these vertebral subluxations.

Chiropractic treatments, called adjustments, manipulate the spine using several hands-on techniques which, while not painful, can be disturbing to watch or to hear. The bones of the body often click and pop as tiny gas bubbles are released in the joints, sometimes rather loudly, as the chiropractor uses their hands to manually twist or manoeuvre the body in a series of specific positions and movements. Other techniques include the use of an activator, which is a hand held spring-loaded device which is pressed and clicked on the body and a drop-table that can be used to swiftly adjust the body's position to a set point.

Chiropractic works well for upper and lower back pain, referred pain, sciatica, headaches and migraines, joint disorders, sports injuries, chronic pain conditions and many other ailments like MS and ME.

Reiki

Reiki healing is a Japanese therapy for relaxation, stress relief and healing. Made up of two words, Rei meaning *universal power* and Ki meaning *life energy* or *life force*, Reiki is literally the power of the universal life-force, channelled through a practitioner during treatments. Dr Mikao Usui, the founder of Reiki healing, was guided to develop the practice in 1922 after years of spiritual development, meditations and retreats. Reiki was brought to the western world by Reiki Master Mrs Takata and the vast majority of Reiki healers in the UK today can trace their teaching back to her. There are three levels of Reiki with each stage or level building on the foundations of the previous – the first level gives the ability to treat oneself, the second is the level of practitioner and the third level is that of Reiki Master or Teacher. Reiki is taught by a series of attunements and students are given a range of symbols that are used to activate Reiki energy and there is an understanding that the healer must first heal oneself and a large emphasis is given on treating the self before treating others. Unlike many other healing disciplines, it will not take years of study to master and become adept at Reiki and this is a great advantage to anyone who lives a busy life and cannot fit in or afford an expensive three year training course or university degree. Reiki is instant and easy and accessible.

Reiki is a very simple healing technique, with the patient remaining fully clothed, either seated or lying down, the practitioner gently places their hand on or slight away from the body in non-intrusive positions. There are key positions up and down the body where the hands are placed, either resting on the body or holding the palms above the body within the energy field of the patient.

Reiki is useful for a wide range of situations and includes emotional healing as well as long or short term physical conditions. Reiki can be used for adults, children, babies and animals and even plants and has a soothing, restorative effect that brings a natural sense of well-being and pace to the whole person, mind, body and soul. The body is capable of healing itself but when we are in a state of dis-ease there is an imbalance between the physical, mental, emotional and spiritual aspects of our being. During a Reiki session, the energy is directed to the parts where it is needed most so that the body can begin or accelerate the healing process. Many physical ailments have underlying emotional causes and this therapy works well in these cases too, bringing a state of harmony and balance, and healing the root cause of the illness as well as the physical symptoms. There are no contra-indications for Reiki and it can be used quite safely alongside 'conventional' medical treatments.

People have benefited from Reiki therapy conditions such as toothache, migraine, arthritis, multiple sclerosis, fibromyalgia, flu and colds, menstrual disorders, endometriosis, headaches, back pain, arthritis and rheumatism and treatments have proved beneficial for long-term and chronic conditions and pain. Pregnant women find it useful for easing the discomfort and aches of pregnancy and babies respond very well to Reiki and it can help to soothe and reduce symptoms like colic or cradle cap. Parents who give Reiki to toddlers have noticed fewer temper tantrums, improved sleeping patterns and it can be soothing and relaxing for children and teens who are going through a difficult time at school or during the stress of intense study periods. Emotional and spiritual healing is a very valuable resource as more and more people are adversely affected by stress and traumatic episodes. Emotional disorders and conditions including addictions, bereavement, paranoia, depression, stress and other, deep rooted, mental health issues and emotional traumas that have built up over the years can all be helped with Reiki. Reiki treatments often give clients a sense of relief and release from negative emotions that have been getting in the way of them living a full and healthy life. Sometimes this is expressed as an immediate sense of release with dramatic effects or as a more subtle release of emotions and healing that takes place during several sessions over a longer period of time.

The energy of Reiki during treatments can sometimes be experienced as a soft tingling sensation. Therapy sessions are set against a background of meditative, relaxing music, soft linens and cushions, the aroma or incense of essential oils and low lighting, but practitioners are trained to 'switch on' their access to Reiki at any time and in any situation. Both I and other Reiki healers I know are able to give and have given treatments on-the-spot when people have asked in the middle of public events like a festival or concert, at the pub or cafe, at a country show or while visiting a friend for social reasons. Reiki can be done distantly too which is great if your Great Uncle Bulgaria in Luton would benefit from some healing while you are in Swansea. Teddy bears, dolls and cushions can all be attuned to act as a substitute for the person who is receiving treatment and the healer uses Reiki symbols to transfer the energy of healing from the substitute to the intended recipient.

Reiki is a defined healing system with specific symbols and attunements to go through along with a period of self-healing and practical sessions before calling oneself a Reiki healer – more simply put, if you have not been attuned to Reiki healing by a Reiki master, whatever healing energy you are accessing, it may be fantastic, but it isn't Reiki. Reiki, unfortunately, has no clearly defined results that can be scientifically proven and this can throw up an element of doubt about its value and effectiveness, especially in light of the placebo effect which shows that if we believe we are being healed, then then we will make ourselves feel better anyway. Whatever the reason for it working, however, that Reiki *does* work is no longer a matter of belief for me, I *know* that Reiki works and here's one example of that which I hope will demonstrate the instinctive way that all creatures react to these subtle-body energies even if we don't consciously understand what is happening.

At home we have three cats, one of whom took to sleeping on a very narrow window ledge for a time. This female cat, aged at least ten years old, previously agile and energetic, was suddenly limping and her back legs sliding out from beneath her if she was startled while running or if she tried to leap and jump about. The vet confirmed our suspicions that she had most likely fallen from the window ledge and injured her back or hips. Medications in the form of steroid injections and pain killers helped a little but after three weeks or so our vet announced that this minor accident had unfortunately triggered the onset of arthritis. The anti-inflammatory drugs he prescribed did not seem to help very much so one evening as the cat curled up on my lap I switched on the flow of Reiki to see if it would help. At once, the cat scarpered and leapt off to go and lick herself elsewhere in the house. However, the following evening, at roughly the same time and in the same place, she came and sat beside me – normally this cat likes to lie on your lap for a fuss so it was unusual behaviour for her to sit at the side of me – she pushed her head against my hands repeatedly and then quickly turned so her back legs were against my hands and miaowed continually until I switched on the Reiki at which point she settled down next to me and purred loudly. After twenty minutes to half an hour she decided enough was enough and off she went. She repeated this the following evening and the next... The results were even clearer when I returned home after a few days away to see her struggling and limping again after four days without her Reiki session. We can't explain to an animal what is happening or what to expect in a way that they understand so having an animal react in such a positive way, demanding Reiki on a regular basis, is a clear indication that this is something more that the placebo effect at work. This evening ritual of Reiki treatments continues almost daily and I firmly believe the cat was at first surprised and startled by the energy flow of Reiki and wondered what on earth was happening and then realised that actually, this energy stuff might be okay after all, let's give it a go! For me, this is a clear demonstration that Reiki healing is effective, even when there is no prior knowledge, hint or suggestion of what can be expected, validating Reiki as something tangible and concrete.

Crystal Healing

Crystal healing therapy works holistically to bring into harmony every aspect of mind, body and spirit. Crystals are essentially igneous rocks and minerals that have been produced through volcanic magma as it cools on its way up through the earth's crust. For example, obsidian crystal is the result of magma cooling so quickly that a crystalline structure doesn't have time to develop and the resulting molten liquid solidifies into a glassy mass. Weathering and sedimentation causes erosion and cracking or splitting of rocks over hundreds or thousands of years and in some cases deposits can build up in these cracks to create a different type of structure or crystal; this includes calcite, selenite and pyrite. Other crystals are formed through the release of gasses or vapours from the magma which then penetrates nearby rocks, leading to a compound rock and gas formation; this would include crystals such as lepidolite, tourmaline and topaz. Crystals come in a wide variety of forms – there are cubic crystals, hexagonal, tetragonal and monoclinic crystal systems or amorphous and orthorhombic crystals, each of which will have slightly different shapes, resonances and qualities. Some crystal healers believe that the intense pressures and changes these rocks and crystalline structures undergo during their formation are representative of the changes and stresses we go through as we progress from birth, through childhood and adulthood and that this provides a solid link for sympathetic healing. Every single type of crystal emits a tiny electrical vibration and using different crystals for different ailments can let these vibrations work to heal the imbalances of the body and soul and help the body to heal itself.

Crystal therapy can help a wide range of physical, mental and emotional problems or symptoms such as migraines and headaches, stress and tension, depression, anxiety, anorexia, digestive disorders, chronic fatigue syndrome, hormonal imbalance, bad habits, addictions, laziness and more. Crystals work by giving off these tiny vibrations or frequencies which interact with imbalances of our psyches, setting things at ease, bringing things into alignment and peace and by channelling energy into our meridian lines and chakras. Crystal healers are adept at selecting one crystal out of hundreds for one person's anorexia while choosing something quite different for another person with same condition, so it is truly a holistic and somewhat intuitive healing process, though some crystals do have a very distinct use while others can work for a wider variety of symptoms and ailments. In addition to the actual crystalline structure used for healing, colours can play an important part in crystal healing too.

Crystals help you access inner peace, a state of balance and being where you will see life for what it really is without judgement, with serenity and peace inside yourself and crystal healers refer to this as living with higher vibrations. Crystals work on a neurological level, their electrical impulses act as circuit breakers to interrupt the negative patterns we have become accustomed to and when used with positive intentions they help us become emotionally free of insecurities and aware of the limitless possibilities life can offer. Crystal healers will help you tune in with nature and the higher vibrational state of mind which adjusts the way you think, leading to instinctive healing, an inner way of knowing what is right for you, releasing old mental programming, allowing you to regain control of your emotions and observing a light hearted attitude blossoming within you, leaving you with peace, balance and harmony within. People turn to crystal healing to help with emotional disorders, stress, depression and anxiety, insomnia, lethargy, menstrual problems, back and muscular pains, hormonal imbalances, colds and flu and for general relaxation which leads to us being more energised and full of vibrant, healthy energy in general.

Crystals come in all shapes, sizes and colours – small polished tumble stones that can be placed on the body, larger pieces which can be held, crystals skulls, crystal eggs or angels, crystal balls, crystal wands that can be used to direct and channel healing energy, pendulums for dowsing and sweeping over the body or activating the chakras, pendants or charms that are worn to give healing energy every time it is worn, a set of seven gems that are placed on the chakras or the very largest pieces of crystal which can be anything from a foot or more high that can remain in the healing room to emit a continual vibration of healing, harmony and relaxation.

There are several associations of complementary healers who offer teaching guides, courses, certificates and diplomas or degrees in crystal healing but there is no overall governing body or defined path of developing crystal therapy. Crystal healing is one of the few complementary healing disciplines that we can try for ourselves as crystals are readily available and unlike herbal medicine there are no contra-indications for therapy and information on how to use crystals is now easy to find. You don't need to cast a formal circle but do set up some kind of healing space with soft lighting, incense and maybe a meditation or healing cd in the background to create a soothing atmosphere, especially if you are treating somebody else.

Chakra Healing Crystal Layout

Sit comfortably and relax – a few minutes or ten of peaceful meditation will help you access the inner mind that is necessary for intuitive healing. Select seven crystals and lie down in a relaxed state and place the crystals on your body against each of the chakra points (if you can, having someone else do this for you will make it a bit easier). Root chakra – a red stone like red jasper, garnet or rhodochrosite; sacral chakra – an orange stone, amber, carnelian or orange calcite; solar plexus – yellow stones, yellow tiger's eye, citrine, yellow fluorite; heart – green crystals like jade, chrysoprase or apophyllite; throat – blue crystals such as blue lace agate, or lapis lazuli; brow – dark blue or purple stones, lepidolite, amethyst or sodalite; crown chakra – white or pale violet crystals such as moonstone, opalite, clear quartz or prehnite. A small piece of black tourmaline or heamatite can be placed between or below the feet as an anchor or grounding crystal. Meditate with the crystals in place, relax and focus on breathing deeply and calmly. Ask mentally that the crystals work to clear you of blockages both in the energy centres and the aura. Mentally see any imbalance being corrected as the crystals work on your chakras to bring healing energy to you. Spend as long as you feel you need to relaxing and working with the energy of the crystals to rebalance your chakras and absorb the energy and vibrations of the crystals.

Crystal Healing

As with the previous crystal session, lay down comfortably and select a few crystals either for their healing properties or colour associations, and place them on or around the body, guided by your intuition. Stay still and silent and breathe deeply, relaxing and meditating while you absorb the healing vibrations of the stones and work them, visualising your pain or illnesses draining away while being replaced with healing, light and love.

Amber - A deep golden colour, not actually a crystal but fossilised tree resin, amber is a good-for-all crystal often used in spells that require success, good luck and happiness, apart from its healing qualities. Provides clarity, confidence, and emotional strength and can be used for eyesight disorders and throat problems.

Amethyst - Purple or violet, amethyst is good for headaches, migraines, stress relief and sleeping difficulties as well as giving feelings of deep relaxation and activating the psychic senses.

Carnelian - A reddish brown or orange coloured crystal, carnelian is good for stabilising blood pressure, an aid to fertility and as an amulet against psychic attack.

Heamatite - A metallic grey or black, this stone stimulates the absorption of iron in the body, restores energy and vitality to the soul and is an excellent grounding crystal.

Jade - A green crystal associated with spiritual well-being, intuitive creativity, dreams, intuition and good for kidney function and balancing the metabolism.

Labradorite - Normally an iridescent blue or green colour, labradorite is a type of feldspar and is known as the illusion killer and highlights forgotten memories, brings us down to earth and stimulates creativity. Physically it is good for colds, fevers and rheumatism.

Lapis Lazuli - Medium to dark blue, often veined, lapis lazuli aids friendships and encourages healthy emotions and communication. Used for harmonising the menstrual cycle, balancing blood pressure and regulating the thyroid.

Moonstone - White or creamy coloured, moonstone encourages lucid dreaming and mediumship abilities while working physically for women's hormonal cycles, childbirth and menopause.

Obsidian - Black or dark brownish in colour, often speckled, this is a good crystal for cleansing negative emotions, treating shock or traumas, alleviating pain, improving circulation and accelerating the healing of wounds.

Prehnite A white or pale green silicate with a rough surface, prehnite is an excellent channel for healing energies and is often used by Reiki therapists to aid the energy flow. Good in itself for cleansing the soul of unpleasant memories, prehnite helps us understand our true nature, stimulates the metabolism, aids the removal of toxins and stimulates the regeneration processes of the body.

Rose quartz A pink crystal associated with love, the heart, emotional healing and fertility. Rose quartz is common as a pendant or earrings and is often found in the shape of hearts or angels. Encourages healthy circulation, stimulates fertility and used in love spells.

Tiger's Eye A type of oxide, tiger's eye is a golden brown colour and is useful for getting through difficult situations, providing courage and inner strength. Physically, it's used for pain relief, anxiety and nervous tendencies.

Staying Healthy

Prevention is definitely better than cure and two of the most crucial ways to stay healthy are diet and exercise. This doesn't mean you have to be working out five days a week and starving yourself of chocolate for the rest of your life, it just means taking some responsibility for your health and being happy with how you are. When we are mentally, emotionally, spiritually and physically healthy, we realise that we do not need, after all, to strive for any of these things that we see in others. We can be content in our own bodies, our own state of mind and being. Relax and enjoy yourself! Of course nobody wants to be ill with either a common cold or a more serious, life threatening disease like cancer or to suffer a heart-attack and there is a lot we can do try and keep ourselves as healthy and vibrant as we possibly can for as long as we can.

A healthy, balanced diet that includes plenty of fresh fruit and vegetables, fibre, proteins including eggs, meat or meat substitutes, nuts, pulses and grains, is going to do everybody good. It doesn't hurt to have things like chocolate, biscuits and sweets in moderation or the odd glass of wine or beer – we don't all have to live like saints and it's in our nature to want those treats from time to time.

Regular exercise is an important part of keeping healthy and not just for weight loss or looks, it will contribute to a healthy heart, good muscle tone and strength, supple joints, wards off osteoporosis, type 2 diabetes and high blood pressure and many, many more physical benefits. Additionally, exercise is a mood enhancer, releasing hormones into the body which can help with depression, anxiety and insomnia and work to reduce stress, increase peaceful feelings and happiness generally and helps us to stay mentally healthy as we age. Even a twenty minute walk twice a week will give you enormous benefits, you don't have to be a body-builder or athlete to be healthy and fit. When I exercise regularly I normally feel vibrant, healthy, full of life and vitality. I feel better mentally and emotionally as well as physically and conversely, when I don't work out for a couple of weeks, I feel more lethargic, bloated, lazy and moody. If you can combine even a little bit of exercise, depending on your physical ability, with a balanced diet, it will promote your ongoing health and happiness.

No matter what your lifestyle choices, however, one of the overriding factors for a long and happy life is your state of mind. People who are happy and content in their lives tend to live longer, have fewer illnesses and are more likely to be living the life they want. Take time out to nurture your spiritual, mental and emotional well-being with things that make you feel happy, with activities you enjoy and with people you love.

CHAPTER 10

Divination

Divination is the art and practice of predicting future events to help people make decisions and to offer advice, insights and intuitions into the questions and problems of life. The subject has a fascinating and lengthy history with some techniques being very recent developments and others dating back to the ancient Egyptians and earlier. Interest in divination shows no signs of waning as more and more people take up the art in one form or another and people from all walks of life, from serving maids to royalty, have paid handsomely for the services of professional psychics, clairvoyants, palmists and card readers.

Some of the earliest methods of fortune telling have impressive histories, coming ancient Egypt, China and Greece, with references to them in ancient sacred texts. Right across the globe people have been curious about the things to come, that great unknown world of the future. Most people who go to a fortune-teller are looking for advice or answers and confirmation that their beliefs and decisions are right.

Sheep knuckles, bones, teeth, human and animal entrails and digging around in animal or human faeces are some of the more bizarre and repulsive things that have been used at one time or another as an aid to divination. We'll see more of these later on – more appealing to the twenty-first century witch are things like the medicine cards, angel cards, rune stones, tea-leaf reading, the ogham, tarot, palmistry and dowsing.

Across Britain we have a wonderful array of simple folklore and traditions that have been used for centuries and persisted during the middle ages when such things were forbidden unless sanctioned by the Church. One example of these country customs is the traditional Samhain apple-bobbing and apple peel throwing still loved by children today. This is a classic example of how divination was, and continues to be, used by ordinary people – apples are particularly associated with romance and were usually used by young ladies to foretell the name of their future husband.

Divination has been used to uncover information about all kinds of subjects with some of the most common being love, health, wealth, marriage, children, money and careers. In addition to predictions about love and marriage, weather was important to our ancestors – a good harvest would not come about without sufficient rain and sun and a particularly harsh winter might literally have been a matter of life or death. It was common for people living in rural areas to be incredibly accurate at foretelling weather patterns by watching cloud formations, bird flight patterns, wind direction and so forth. While some of these gentle divinatory practices have died out, there are still people around who remember them and carry on watching the sky for portents and their animals for omens.

Our ancestors passed onto us not only some of the knowledge and language of their ways but also their curiosity about the future. The guarantee of getting rain or shine may not be such an important issue to the majority of people any more, but matters of love and marriage, careers, wealth and health are certainly things with which we are concerned today and turning to fortune tellers to find some insight into these big issues can be comforting and reassuring.

Clients often ask: *What should I do about this situation?* I feel it is the reader's job to offer their insights and intuition but not to tell people which course of action to take. Divination is by no means an absolute science but some people think it can give all the answers. It's only a guideline though, not a text book - let the client know if you have a particular image or message for them, but they should draw their own conclusions about their future actions. Nobody should make decisions based on the reading alone; divination offers clarification, guidance and insights and as oracle readers we have a responsibility to give knowledge and advice which will be beneficial and helpful in guiding our clients to draw their own conclusions.

Divination is growing in popularity in the collective consciousness with the advent of horoscope columns in the daily papers and the growing trend of psychic fairs. In addition to professional readers, there is a huge market for DIY prediction. Rune sets and tarot cards are available in even the most conservative of mainstream bookstores. Angel cards, medicine wheel cards, vampire tarot or fairy rune sets are popular in new-age shops and there are more springing up every day – there's even a zombie tarot. Ones that always amuse me are the ogham or rune tarot cards – is it Ogham, is Runes or is it Tarot? They are all very different with both ogham and runes having very little in common with the tarot or even with each other and neither the ogham or runes would have been made into a deck of cards in their original time period. Certainly the various cards and casting sets are delightful and beautiful to own, if a little impersonal due to their mass-marketing and the predetermined list of exact interpretations. Yet there is no reason at all why these should be any more or less effective than any other method. The finest tool of prediction however, has to be seen first and foremost as the intuitive mind of the reader. All the cards and bones in the world will not determine the future or uncover the past without a reader who can interpret the signs and see past the symbolism to the truth of the matter at hand.

Predictive readings can be done to some degree of accuracy by anyone with a deck of cards or a palm to examine, however, while anyone can tell you what a certain card or a particular line on the crease of your hand is supposed to mean by looking it up in a book, not everyone will be able to get consistently good or accurate results that are relevant to their client.

The information and intuitions we receive while carrying out a prediction or reading cannot be said to come from one definite source or another with any degree of certainty. Some people think it comes from the 'other side', the realm of the Beloved Dead; others believe it comes from the collective unconsciousness or the energies of Wyrd; some people believe they tap into a psychic telephone line to the subject's subconscious mind; some are of the opinion that they are using precognition to actually see future events before they happen. Still others don't have any firm ideas of the source, but know through experience that wherever it comes from, it just works – after reading tarot cards for some twenty-five years and more recently the ogham, I still include myself in that last category.

There are literally hundreds of divination techniques to be explored and if you have the time, patience and resources, you might like to conduct your own research into some of the more appealing ones, be it the tarot, runes, ogham, tasseomancy or palmistry. Learning to develop your psychic skill in conjunction with your growing knowledge about the tools you use takes time and practice and comes more easily to some people than others, but with practice, patience and persistence everybody can develop their intuition.

The Divination Directory

Some of the ancient forms of divination seem might weird and disgusting when compared to the standard cards or runes used today. Here is a quick guide to just a few of the methods that have been practiced in the past and some of those still used. Please note that the more weird, unusual and sometimes grotesque practices listed here are included as a point of interest only!

Animal Divination

The behaviour of animals may not be of particular interest to anyone who lives in the city but there are still people in rural areas who know that when cows lie down in the fields it indicates rain or that a swan flexing its head and neck backwards over folded wings signals thunder.

Ailuromancy 'Ailuro' is the Greek word meaning 'cat' and this type of divination interprets the movements, colours, behaviours and temperaments of cats. A black cat can be either bad or good luck, depending on where you live, and a sneezing cat indicates rain. Also called felidomancy.

Apiomancy relates to bees and their habits. Beekeepers must always talk to their bees, letting them know of births, deaths and marriages in the family to keep the honey sweet and to stop bees from leaving the hive and a piece of wedding cake must be left out for the bees. A single bee in your house brings good news while a bee landing on a dead tree signals death or bad news.

Batraquamancy uses frogs for divination – British folklore states that if you rub a live frog over a wart, the wart will disappear. Frogs have been used both alive, dead and dried for divination.

Hippomancy is the observation of horses and their movements. Horses often represent travel or strength of character when seen in dreams. The colour, size, movements and noises of the horse can all be seen as indicators of misfortune or good luck. Two horses walking away from each other might indicate arguments, for example. If horses walk away from you it indicates a journey.

Myomancy is a type of zoomancy using rats and mice. An observer notices their behaviours, physical appearance, locations and movements and assigns them symbolic meanings. **Myrmomancy** is concerned with ants, live ones, and particularly their eating habits.

Nggàm - Practised by the Mambila tribe of Nigeria and Cameroon, this technique involves a shallow bowl or depression in the ground filled with various objects or cards. A spider or crab is let into the bowl. The creature moves about and disturbs the contents and then fortunes are told and decisions made based on the displacement of the objects.

Ornithomancy is bird divination. The breed and size of the bird, the number of birds, the direction of flight, flock formations, bird calls and more are indicators of practically any event you care to name. From tomorrow's weather to next week's illness, it was all seen in the world of birds.

Scapulomancy – another type animal divination, Scapulomancy takes the scapulae, or shoulder bones, of a sacrificial beast for analysis. It is usually done with the burned bones of deer and pigs, with the seer examining the cracks and patterns in the charred bone.

Zoomancy is the generic name for the study of animals for divination through observation of their behaviours and random encounters with animals. For example, a house martin brings good luck to any house where it nests and rears its young, a rabbit running down your street indicates a death and bats flying into your house indicate a death in the family.

The Casting of Lots

Throwing a selection of randomly chosen dice, bones, sticks or stones onto the floor, table or casting cloth, turns what should be a chance arrangement into something more meaningful and open to interpretation. The casting of lots could use anything from a bag of coloured jelly beans to a hand-crafted set of runes passed down through generations – it's not what you use but how you read it.

Astragalomancy is the study of either numbered or lettered dice for interpretation and dates back to at least 500 BC. Originally the dice were made from the astragli (knuckle) bones of sheep and goats.

Cleromancy is not a form of divination in itself but is the generic name for the casting or throwing of lots, stones, beads, sticks or bones for the purpose of divination.

Jelly Bean-omancy – take a bag of brightly coloured jelly beans (or similar multi-coloured sweets) and throw a few in front of you. Look at which colours lie close together, closer to you, near the edge of the table and apply meanings to the beans according to colour and position and see if it makes some kind of sense when you put it together. Jelly bean-omancy is entirely made-up for this book, of course, but that doesn't mean it won't work if you try it. I think it illustrates perfectly how adaptable and full of humour witches can be – everything can be meaningful if we open up our intuition.

Lithomancy traditionally uses thirteen precious stones or crystals thrown by the questioner. A casting cloth is used, with areas marked out for health, wealth etc. and the placement of the gems and stones in the different locations gives the reader the information.

Ogham is a form of cleromancy using symbols carved onto small wooden sticks or staffs. Ogham is the Celtic tree alphabet and unlike runes which form distinct, individual characters, the Ogham are short lines made on a continuous horizontal line, etched into slim wooden sticks. There is no real evidence, to date, that the ogham was ever used as an oracle by the Celts though druids and other pagans today often use them to gain insights and there are even couple of Ogham card decks available. Better still, if you are interested in the Ogham, is to gather small twigs (fallen branches are best to avoid damaging any living trees) of each of the twenty trees and carve or engrave them with the associated tree symbol.

Rhabdomancy – the casting of sticks or rods onto the ground or a casting cloth to produce meaningful patterns and shapes from which information and insights can be gained.

Runes - Futhark or Germanic runes are a set of angular symbols etched into small pieces of wood or stone. The symbols are said to have been seen by the Norse all-father god Odin as he hung for nine days and nine nights from the world tree, Ygdrassil. Odin looked down on the last day and saw the rune shapes lying on the ground and developed them as a form of communication. There are twenty-four runes, normally painted or carved into wood or stone and picked out of a bag by the querent for interpretation.

Fire Divination

There are few things more entrancing than the flickering flames of an open fire, especially out of doors at night. The flames seem to dance and flicker, the wood burns and spits in captivating ways and the smoke rises up to the skies in swirls and flurries. Fire has long been used for divination and when you have been sitting around a camp fire in the evening, perhaps after a glass or two of wine with good friends or after a Sabbat ritual, it's easy to see why.

Knissomancy involves burning incense and watching the patterns made by the smoke as it drifts around in the air.

Lampadomancy is the use of flaming torches or oil lamps and interpreting the flickering flames and rising smoke patterns. There are certain stipulations to be observed, such as the type of oil used and the time of day or night when the fortune telling is carried out.

Pyromancy is the collective name for divination through the medium of fire. Candles, torches, lamps and open fires are alive with fire spirits and almost universally, we are drawn to gaze at the flickering shapes formed in open fires. Regardless of spiritual orientation we are captivated by it and the way it flickers, moves and glows. Wood, bones, cloth, plants and paper have all been used in pyromancy and the ash and embers can be looked at as well as the flames themselves as the objects burn.

Food and Drink

There are hundreds of little customs and traditions of fortune telling through the medium of food and drink. Some of them are still used regularly in the home and could really be classed as superstitions or omens, rather than divination. For example, spilling salt has to be followed by throwing a pinch of it over your shoulder to ward off bad luck. Christmas puddings are filled with trinkets – a ring, a coin, a key, a locket – to predict different things for the person whose portion of pudding contains them. Apple bobbing is a throwback to an old custom where the initials of eligible young men were carved into apples which were floating in the water. Apple peel, carefully peeled in a long, continuous strip, can be thrown over the shoulder and the letter formed by the peel when it lands is supposed to represent the initial of the person you will end up marrying. All very well if you know lots of people with the initial 'C' or 'S'. By brushing your hair and eating an apple in front of a mirror at midnight on Samhain eve, you conjure up in the mirror an image of your intended spouse.

Cromniomancy is fortune telling with the humble onion. Two onions, each representing a potential suitor, are planted and the first one to sprout will indicate which suitor the fair maid will marry. Onions can also be peeled, looking for patterns or oddities in the skins and layers that might be classed as an omen.

Oinomancy examines wine spilled on cloth or the sediment in the bottle. Usually done by a Priestess (known as a Bacchante) of Bacchus, the god of wine, the interpretations were preceded by drinking of large quantities of wine – whether this led on to accurate prophecies or not and whether it was remembered the next morning is anybody's guess!

Oomancy uses eggs and may have taken the place of extispicy as it became outdated and unpopular. Eggs can be broken into a bowl of water to see patterns and forms or kept whole and the shell examined for omens of upcoming events. Eggs can be used to predict if a pregnant woman would have a boy or girl. She has to incubate an egg in her bosom until it hatches and the gender of the chick will indicate the sex of her baby.

Tasseography (tea-leaf reading) has been around for a long time, dating back to ancient Greece and Asia. While it still practiced today, it's has become less common, due mainly to the advent of tea-bags. There are particular directions in which to stir the tea and turn the cup and further directions for the type of tea and amount of leaves used. The shapes and forms the leaves settled into are taken as symbols to interpret, such as a cross or a hand. A friend of mine does this with ground coffee and with good results.

Tiromancy/Tyromancy involves using spoiled and rotting cheese for intuitive insights.

Nature and the Earth

It's nice to see that some remnants of the old ways still exist today – even urbanites know some of the phrases that used to be common: When the wind is from the east, it's neither good for man nor beast. There are countless country beliefs like this one relating to weather, animals, health, death, disaster, weddings or good fortune. Pine cones hanging up to predict rain by opening or closing up or a swarm of bees landing on the walls of a house indicating a death are more examples of the simple ways in which nature told the future.

Botanomancy involves burning plants – specifically the leaves and branches of herbs and trees – the interpretation comes from observing the plants as they burned. Although it has its own name, this is really one of the many forms of Pyromancy.

Floriography gathers information and messages from the natural appearances of flowers: colours, numbers of petals and locations of the plants were important. If you were given flowers in the early middle ages, they were more than a mere gift – they gave you a message from the sender. Red roses were a symbol of passion, ivy meant faithfulness, sunflowers were for happiness and the garden daisy stands for purity and innocence.

Hydromancy uses the medium of water, seeing visions of the future or past in the reflections on the water's surface. There are a variety of different techniques employed such as dropping pebbles into still or running water and watching the concentric ripples as they spread out or putting a drop of oil into a goblet of water to create a mirror in which to see the future. It could also mean gazing into the depths of a clear pool, interpreting the flow, colour and waves in the sea or a river or even getting meaningful intuitions while you enter that switched-off state of mind as you do the washing up – one witch friend of mine has had this happen spontaneously on several occasions.

Nephomancy is the study of cloud formations for divination. Colours, shapes, direction, speed of movement and location in the sky are all relevant. Spirits of the dead were sometimes asked to project images and pictures of the future onto the clouds for interpretation.

Xylomancy is the chance appearance of wood or wooden objects with significant meanings and also the burning of wood to obtain an interpretation from the flames.

Divination through People

Not content with the study of external phenomena, we have come up with a wealth of techniques and traditions for gathering information and predicting future events based on or around the human body. Some of them are lovely little quirks that your grannie might know and others are less appealing.

Amniomancy involves the caul or membrane surrounding a new born baby for colour, consistency and vibrancy to predict how the child's life will turn out.

Chiromancy is perhaps better known as Palmistry. A chiromancer looks at the lines, markings and shapes of the hands and palms to predict the future and give information about the general life of the querent. Palmistry is one of the ancient arts with references to it in the Vedic scripts and early Semitic writings. It was used in India around 2-3000 years BC and was first recorded in Europe in the twelfth century. Hippocrates and Galen both used palmistry as a health reference and of course it has long been associated with Romany fortune-tellers. It isn't just the lines of the hand which are important; a good palm reader will also take account of the skin colour and texture, the shape of the fingers, the ridges, shape and condition of the nails, the hair on the hands and even the way you hold your palm when resting.

Dactylomancy is carried out by suspending rings on a length of thread or ribbon over a chart, picture, or book. Often, the thread would be burned through and the words or symbols on which the ring landed could be picked out and the reading taken from those. The wedding ring of a pregnant woman is dangled over her stomach to indicate if the baby is going to be a boy or girl. This is one of the tried and tested folk customs which has not quite died out yet but the trouble is that although your mother or her mother might have done it years ago, if you ask her to do it for you now, she'll be blowed if she can remember which way meant boy and which way meant girl!

Geloscopy is the study of human speech through tonality, pace and resonance of the voice and, most importantly of all, the sound of laughter. The more hysterical the laughter, the better the results.

Gyromancy encourages a volunteer to spin round and round in circles until they are so dizzy they either fall over or pass out. The reading is then achieved by looking at how, when and in what way they have fallen, often within a defined area which marks out the possible outcomes of a situation.

Ichnomancy is the reading and study of footprints, observing the posture, position, stride and depth of the print.

Odontomancy, as the name suggests, uses the teeth of animals or humans in an effort to predict future events. Teeth are extracted and the discolorations, markings and chips on them can be interpreted.

Omphaomancy is quite literally navel gazing. A new born baby's umbilicus and navel was examined to reveal the number and gender of children the baby would have as an adult.

Phrenology is the examination of the head and the bumps of the skull. Phrenology was considered something of a science in its heyday and used the same model of the head as once used by the medical profession; if you see a white, porcelain head with little black numbers and lines painted on, it would most likely have had a dual purpose as a medical teaching tool and as a model of reference for Phrenology.

Podomancy (sometimes called Solistry) uses another body part thankfully not extracted or dissected, but merely examined. It involved the close up detail of the feet; the shape of them, the lines and textures of the soles, the shape of the feet and the walking pattern of the individual.

Sternomancy uses the bumps, lumps and shape of the sternum for interpretation.

Xenomancy is the chance movements, interactions and meetings with strangers as interpreted for divination. This could be overhearing a random conversation or bumping into someone accidentally.

The Gruesome Ones

Anthropomancy involves the observation and study of the entrails and innards of a dying or sacrificed person.

Dririmancy ovserves the dripping of blood as an animal or human sacrifice is killed and interpreting the patterns it makes as it gushes and spatters into a goblet or on the ground.

Extispicy is the practice of using the entrails of dead animals for divination. Ritually sacrificed and purified animals are used and the divination is carried out immediately afterwards, with anomalies or unusual features of the entrails deemed relevant to interpretation.

Haruspices (sometimes called **Hepatoscopy**) is a form of extispicy, specifically using the livers of ritually sacrificed animals. Carried out by an officiating Priest, known as the Haruspex, there were set rituals and procedures that had to be performed to get auspicious readings.

Ichthyomancy is another form of extispicy, this time with the medium of fish entrails.

Scatomancy is the art of prediction by means of faeces – the colour, consistency, content, texture.

Spatilomancy same as above but uses animal faeces. Remember the old saying that having bird poo land on you is a sign of good luck? This type of fortune telling takes that a step or two further and reaches to the extremes of smelling and poking at the animal's offering and sometimes even tasting it.

Urimancy is urine examination. The colour, taste, scent and flow are observed as well as the presence and patterns of bubbles in the pot.

An A – Z of the Rest

Arithmancy – forget Hogwarts, this is just another word for Numerology.

Astrology is one you will be familiar with through the daily horoscope column now appearing in almost all known newspapers. Astrologers collate information about star signs, moon signs, rising planets, planetary houses, eclipses, conjunctions and much more detail than you can shake a stick at. Astrology has been with us for thousands of years – as we know, some of the oldest civilisations could chart the progress of the planets and stars through the night sky. Sun signs are the most commonly known feature of astrology but there are many more aspects which combine to give often uncannily accurate predictions.

Axinomancy is the practice of throwing an axe or hatchet at the ground or against a tree and predictions are taken from the way the blade quivers or the direction in which the handle points. The type of wood used for the axe handle, the tree it landed in and the metal used for the axe-head were irrelevant – it was the final position of the axe that was taken into account for divination.

Bibliomancy is not the study of the bible for prediction but of books in general. Any book can used, opened to a completely random page and the querent lets his or her finger wander randomly over the page and stops it anywhere. Reading the passage of the book where the finger stops is meant to give meaningful information.

Cartomancy refers to any type of card reading although it is usually used now in relation to someone who uses a conventional deck of fifty-two playing cards. These are ordinarily laid out in a quite a large display of face-up cards to give the reader the information.

Clairvoyance is the psychic ability of seeing future events before they happen. Clairvoyance literally means clear seeing while Clairaudience is clear hearing. A clairvoyant, can see or hear (sometimes both) a vision of future events or a stream of significant images. Some clairvoyants can see emotions and situations through holding an object; a watch or wedding band (see Psychometry). Clairvoyants are often mediums and spiritualists. This degree of psychic ability or second-sight tends to run in families, often through the female line, but it can also occur spontaneously.

Crystallomancy, as the name suggests, refers to crystal gazing and is a form of scrying. The traditional image of an old woman wearing flowing robes and asking you to cross her palm with silver before looking into a gigantic, flawless crystal, is far from being realistic. True crystals of that size are few and far between and a large crystal without flaws is even rarer. I have three small crystal balls and find the flaws and shapes within them add to, rather than detract from, the experience of scrying. Large, clear crystals are incredibly expensive so glass is often used instead usually giving good results.

Dowsing can be carried out with either a pendulum or with a pair of dowsing rods and relies on external forces or energies to give answers through the movement of the tool. Dowsing rods are 'L' shaped with the short end held loosely in the hands to allow free movement of the longer end. Pendulums can be crystals or rings hung on chains or a special, pointed pendulum called a witness, which has a cavity inside for holding a sample of the object you want to find. Dowsers can locate missing items, find water sources and answer questions. There is a great demand in some industries, including the building, water and oil trades, for accurate dowsers to find suitable locations for mining, drilling or building. Answers are interpreted according to the movement of the dowsing rods or pendulum, indicating a positive or negative response.

I Ching, meaning 'book of changes', is an ancient Chinese method of divination, reportedly dating back as far as 2850 BC and only brought to the Western continents in the nineteenth century. It uses sixty-four hexagrams laid out in trigrams of three broken and unbroken lines, the broken lines being the Yin or female symbols and the solid lines representing the Yang or masculine. The I Ching is cast by throwing three coins three times and reading the hexagrams from a book of interpretations.

Jnana is the eastern art of gaining knowledge through deep meditation.

Ka-Bala, developed in 1967, this mass-produced board game, manufactured from glow-in-the-dark green plastic was essentially a game of chance. A black marble spins round a track and lands on 'yes' or 'no' to answer questions. There were also options to get the ball to generate horoscopes and tarot readings using the Major Arcana cards provided with the game.

Necromancy refers not to dead bodies, but to their spirits. The souls of the departed are summoned up and questioned. As they are considered to be closer to the divine than those still living, it is assumed that their information would be more accurate and useful. Necromancy was not the same as medium-ship; the necromancer invoked and called up the spirits at their command, rather than communicating with them clairvoyantly. Certain rules are obeyed concerning the time, place and manner in which the spirits are summoned. Magical symbols and circles are drawn on the floor to protect the necromancer from evil spirits.

Numerology uses a wide range of different charts to assign each letter of the alphabet a number, a numerologist can transform your name, date of birth, place of residence and other information, into a number or series of numbers. The digits of numbers greater than nine, with a few exceptions, are added together to make a single figure total. A fascinating subject, numerology can tell if you are compatible with your house, your job, your partner, and also gives predictions of future events.

Oneiromancy is dream interpretation. Interpretation is gained through examining the archetypes, symbols and images that appear in our dreams. There are dream dictionaries galore on the bookstore shelves, though they are sometimes contradictory. Dream interpretation can be done on a more personal level, potentially with more success. Decide what issue you need clarification on and tell yourself that you will dream up a solution. Write down anything you remember happening or any feelings you have regarding the dream. Even something vague, like a colour, or the mood of a dream can be used. Think about what this means for you and compare your intuitions with classic interpretations and see which fits the question you want answering. Dreams really can be prophetic and many mystics and psychics have correctly predicted events that have taken place at a later date.

Querent is the client asking the questions, as opposed to the person doing the reading.

Scrying is not so much a practice on its own but the general art of seeing visions or getting deep intuitions through the medium of any reflective surface. It includes hydromancy, crystallomancy and the witches' mirror among others.

Sortilege is not a form of divination in its own right but just refers to the casting of lots in general.

Tarot dates back to ancient Egypt or earlier and consists of seventy-eight picture cards divided into one suit of named Major Arcana and four suits of numbered Minor Arcana. The four suits are cups, wands (or staves), swords and coins (or pentagrams). Together, the five suits represent the five elements. The tarot is widely accepted as an accurate method of divination and is one of the most popular mediums. By spreading the cards in particular layouts, the reader can determine the course of events past, present and future. There are literally hundreds of different packs of tarot cards being used, from the Rider-Waite deck, first published in 1909, to the modern decks which include things like the Witches' tarot, the Silicon Valley tarot or the medicine wheel cards to name but a few.

Uranomancy, observing the 'heavens;' literally meaning the sky in general and its atmospheric changes as well as any objects appearing in the sky (but does not include astronomy).

Vaticinia de Summis Pontificibus is a series of illustrated prophecies dating to around 1280 during the years of Pope Nicholas 3rd. Its prophecies relate to the chronology of the Papacy.

Witch Mirrors, hand-made by witches or elaborately carved and adorned for a small fortune in a new-age shop, the witch mirror is a black mirror used for scrying. The mirror will normally be placed into a wooden frame and kept covered while not in use. Alternatively, the mirror can be a black bowl filled with water to give a reflective surface with a depth to it. A witch mirror can be a piece of concave glass, like an old clock-face turned over and placed inside a frame or box lined with black cloth. The mirror's surface (or the water) becomes a screen for visions and images.

Zodiac, meaning 'circle of animals.' The twelve signs of the zodiac comprise 30° of longitude each, making up a band of the heavens above earth. Aries, Taurus, Gemini, Cancer, Leo, Virgo, Libra, Scorpio, Sagittarius, Capricorn, Aquarius and Pisces make up the circle of animals and each planet in our solar system has an influence on earthly events as it passes through the constellations. The zodiac is used, along with other astrological bodies, in astrology

Divination Stones

Predicting the future does not have to involve complicated and ancient traditions of cards, pictograms or entrails. Tarot, runes, the ogham or palmistry can be useful as we learn the symbols and meanings of them but divination with complex tools can take a lot of time, study and patience to achieve. It might be better start your forays into the world of divination with something more personal, such as a set of symbols that you create yourself which have an easily accessible meaning that you can recognize straight away. Coming up with a set of unique symbols to use for divination can be an effective way of switching on your psychic ability to get accurate and positive readings, without the long study needed to really grasp the all the subtle and complex interpretations of something like the tarot.

If this is something you would like to try out, you should find it easy enough to gather about fifteen to twenty small pebbles to create a set of stones for casting. A square of fabric can be your casting cloth if you want to use one; paint it with circles to represent areas like the past, present or future, health, finances and relationships.

Preparation…

For one month before you make these stones, talk with the moon and sun energy, ask the elements of earth, air, fire, water and spirit for inspiration and insight regarding the symbols you will use and the interpretations you want them to portray. Think about what you would want to know if you were consulting an oracle and how this information could be captured in a symbolic representation.

Divination commonly concerns the following topics and the various issues involved with each; money and wealth; health and sickness; career and stress; love and betrayal; children and fertility; family and the home; peace and happiness.

What your symbols will look like is a matter of preference. Your own personal symbols for the subjects you want to cover can be given to you by your guide or by asking for them during deep meditation or journey. Before making the stones or carrying out a journey for relevant symbolism, you can refer to various books or search the internet for meaningful symbols to give you inspiration. Perhaps they will occur to you out of the blue, when your mind is on something completely different or you could include any ancient or occult symbols that seem relevant. It could be a completely random shape or line, a pair of parallel lines, a triangle inside a square or the outlined shape of a bird in flight. The symbols don't have to be unique or wonderfully artistic when painted onto the stones – they only have to be a representation; you could just paint a blob of colour if it means something significant to you.

Some ideas for what to include on your stones are given below but whatever you decided to use, remember you are the only person who needs to recognise both the symbol and the meaning behind it. Be creative and follow your intuition.

Meaning	**Suggested Symbol**
Lovers	joined rings, a heart shape
Money	gold or silver coloured circle, the £ sign
Strength	antlers, Thor's hammer, an oak leaf
Growth	seed or corn, a flower
Legal matters	a gavel, paper
Good fortune	the sun, an overflowing cup
Bad fortune	waning moon crescent, an 'x' cross
Health	full moon circle, the caduceus

Children	new moon crescent, skipping rope, rattle
Birth/Extreme good luck	a cradle, a shooting star, a diamond
Death/Extreme bad luck	a coffin, a scythe, a snake, a lightning bolt
House/home-life	a house, a nest, keys, a door
Travel	a boat, plane or car
Career	a spade, a diamond
Enemies	a bullet, bow and arrow
Arguments/Problems	arrows pointing in opposite directions, a knife
Friends	joined hands, a dog
Man/Woman	the male/female signs, yin/yang symbols
Sorrow/Grief	tear drops, a waterfall
Happiness	the sun, a smiling face

About a week or so before you intend to decorate and consecrate the stones, find a place where you are likely to find some – take a country walk or go beach combing – and collect a handful of pebbles or stones of similar size and shape. Take care not to disturb any natural habitats in the process. Be open to the possibility of finding yourself wandering off course while listening to the call of your inner guidance to collect the stones that feel right. You might even find stones that have a hint of relevant colours or are shaped in a meaningful way. When you have enough, wash them to remove any dirt and carry out a cleansing by covering the stones with sea-salt or immersing them in water for twenty-four hours. Leave them on your windowsill to benefit from the light of the sun and the energy of the moon.

The ritual…

Choose a full moon night for your ritual to enhance the energy and magic and prepare your notes, paints, brushes, stones and your usual circle casting paraphernalia if you have any. You will also need two squares of soft fabric and some ribbon to make a pouch and a casting cloth. Gather up anything else you might need to embellish the finished stones and pouch. Ritually cleanse all these items before use with a smudge bundle or try another method of cleansing that works for you; ringing a bell to shake away unwanted energy, for example.

Create your sacred space and invite the elements and goddess and god to be present. Spread out your equipment and spend a few minutes in meditation to reflect on the task before you. Ask each element in turn for its blessing and to help you as you create and consecrate the stones.

Pick up the first stone and hold it in both hands, try to sense what its energy is like. Clear your mind and pick up on what it is telling you. Your intuitions and instincts will help you decide what this particular stone will represent; first impressions are usually the most reliable. Once you are clear about what this stone means, choose a symbol you think will be appropriate and again meditate on which symbol the stone lends itself to most readily. Is this the right shape for a certain sigil, the right colour or texture?

Now go ahead and paint the symbol on this stone straight away before moving on to the next and repeating the process. Even if you have a carefully planned notebook full of ideas for your stones, tapping into their individual energy and working with it will give you an even fuller understanding of their meaning and will help you give a more useful reading when you come to use the stones.

When you have been through all the stones you need, leave the paint to dry while you prepare your casting cloth. The casting cloth doesn't need to have any markings on it, though you might prefer to use markings as guide when starting out. As a suggested layout, use fabric pens or embroidery thread to put a circle in the centre of the cloth, with four more circles of equal size around the outside of this one. The colour of each circle should represent one of the five elements, with the spirit circle being in the centre. You could also draw circles to represent health, finances, relationships, future or past events. Make sure the edges of the cloth will not fray by sewing a thin hem all the way round. If your sewing skills are limited, iron on some adhesive hemming tape to secure the hem instead or use leather, suede or fleece fabrics to eliminate the need for a hem at all.

Make a pouch by cutting a second circle of fabric and with the stones in the centre, gather up the edges and tie it closed with a ribbon or cord. Hold up the cloth, pouch and stones to each of the elements and the goddess and god in turn, asking each one to contribute their blessing to the stones as a tool for guidance and prophecy.

Close up your sacred space, giving thanks as appropriate and leave the stones, pouch and casting cloth on the windowsill where the moonlight and sunlight can fall on them without disturbance for one whole moon cycle.

Your intuition might tell you to use the stones straight away or maybe your symbols and stones were already clear as you picked them up on the path. Go ahead and do whatever you feel is right, as with everything in witchcraft, you will get the best results by following your gut instincts – only you know what is right for you.

Casting the Stones

Spread the casting cloth and select a stone without looking, placing it at random anywhere on the cloth. Pay attention both to its meaning and its position on the casting cloth. If a stone is placed on or very close to an element circle, it relates to that aspect of your life. Fire (a red circle) represents love, anger, ambition, passion and goals; Earth (a green or brown circle) represents the home, family, children, animals, possessions and material matters; Water (a blue circle) can represent the emotions, balance, harmony and life-cycles; Air (a yellow or white circle) represents the intellect, careers, tests, education and communication; Spirit (the centre circle) represents the soul, the energy surrounding the issue and the inner state of the person you are reading for.

Interpretation is very much a matter of using your intuition and instincts. As stated earlier, first impressions are usually correct. If you have a gut instinct that a move up the career ladder is in store for someone, trust your instincts and nine times out of ten, you'll be right. Lay another stone on the cloth and again, place it wherever it seems to draw you, think about the meaning of the second stone and how it might relate to the first. Placing stones close together indicates they are linked but if they are further apart then the issues are either unrelated or opposing each other. If one stone seems to jump out of the pouch, put it on the cloth immediately as it is likely to be a key issue in the reading, perhaps something you need to act on straight away. If you drop a stone on the floor, it should also be placed on the cloth, this could be another key issue, possibly something you need to let go of or get rid of.

Store the stones safely when not in use and cleanse them from time to time as you start to do readings for other people. As with any magical or energy work, the elements and deities you called on to begin with should be given thanks when you finish.

Write down anything you find relevant as and when it comes up during a reading. If you are reading the stones for someone else, they, not you, should take the stones out of the bag and position them on the cloth at random. There are other ways of selecting the stones for a reading. You could pick out several stones and cast them onto the cloth all at once, select a specific number of stones to represent particular issues or pick out a single stone in the morning to represent your day ahead.

Witch Mirrors

The witch mirror can be an ordinary household or make-up mirror specially bought and consecrated for magical work or it can be a unique hand-crafted mirror set in an ornate frame. There are some very beautiful scrying mirrors available to buy but as with everything in the craft, choosing, buying or making a mirror is a matter of personal taste, budget and craftsmanship. For example, my own crafting skills don't go so far as woodworking but I can sew my own robes or tarot pouches. There are some very talented craftspeople in the Pagan community who make working tools at a fair price so it's worth looking around and talking to people to see what you can find.

A witch mirror can be made from a piece of concave glass painted black on the reverse and mounted in a frame. It should be fairly easy to get hold of an old clock from a junk shop or jumble sale quite cheaply so that you can use the domed glass face of it as a mirror. Clean it well and give the convex side two or three coats of black paint before fixing it into a frame. If you have basic DIY skills, you can make your own box, if not, find a ready-made box to use as a base, even an old shoe-box would do to start with. Line with foam padding or cotton wool to get a snug fit and protect the glass. Cover the padding with black silk or velvet and then sink the glass into place on top of this. The lid should also be padded for protection and again covered in black fabric. The box can be painted and decorated with sigils, pentacles and runes or left blank according to personal taste and preference.

Another easy way of making a witch mirror is by filling a black or other dark coloured bowl with water and using the water as the scrying surface. Try scrying in water with a floating candle in a traditional iron cauldron; it doesn't have to be a large one. Consecrate the mirror before you use it for the first time and keep it wrapped up in dark cloth when not in use.

Scrying…

To use the mirror, cast a sacred circle as normal and have the room as dark as possible, with just one or two candles set on the altar, so that there is no direct light reflected on the glass. Ask the Old Ones to give you clear sight and visions.

Make yourself comfortable with the mirror either in your hands or on the altar. Relax and clear your mind. Soften your gaze and look into the mirror. After a while and with a bit of luck images may appear in it. Anything you see might come and go at first but with practice and patience it should become clearer and steadier. Keep your mind relaxed and unfocused, if you try too hard to see things in the glass you are not likely to have much luck – a relaxed and meditative, dreamy state of mind is best for scrying. The first time you practice scrying with your mirror, you might find that nothing happens and this is quite normal. It often takes many attempts to get even the vaguest of images coming through so if at first you don't succeed...

It is worth bearing in mind that scrying is not restricted to what we see. Not everybody receives information as visual images; some people are clairaudient – better at hearing messages, others will be more clairsensitive and will pick up on the emotions surrounding an issue. Some people can also sense tastes or smells through scrying. It's quite common, however, to get a deep sense of just 'knowing' something. Record anything that does come through straight away in your Book of Shadows and when you have finished, close the circle as normal.

Practice Pays Off

You have probably gathered by now that accurate divination happens more through intuition than through memorising the symbols, signs and omens written into the cards or stones. There are no hard and fast rules or interpretations involved. If you give a reading for someone else, perhaps you might be worried that your predictions weren't quite right but what really matters is that people feel better when the reading is finished than they did before it started. Not everybody has psychic or clairvoyant ability but with practice, persistence, patience and more practice, you should stand a good chance of being right more often than not as your psychic muscles get used to the exercise.

It is not always practical or necessary to cast a full circle when you carry out divination, but it is important to approach the reading with the right frame of mind – that is, a relaxed and open mind. It is always worth taking a few moments to still your mind and silently ask the goddess and god to give you accurate and helpful information.

With any method of divination, the intuition and natural psychic abilities of the reader play an important part in the interpretation. Try and be aware throughout the session of your intuition coming into play by relaxing into a state of enhanced awareness, asking the Old Ones to help you say the right things. See if you can expand on what you have learned about your chosen divinatory tool, be it tarot, stones, pendulum or scrying, by adding to the bare facts with your own insights.

Everyone has their own way of tapping into their intuitive voice such as creating sacred space, using a specific incense blend or repeating a mantra. Try this one or make up something of your own and see if it helps.

Horned One, Crescent One, give to me,
The insights that I need to see.
Let the secrets be imparted,
Let the truth be now unveiled.
With all the power of earth and sea,
As I do will, so mote it be.

As you practice, your intuition will start to develop and you can begin to investigate some of the ways our ancestors predicted things; by looking at the way a fish moves in the water or taking the random messages of rustling trees as a portent. The key to all of this, no matter what method of divination you use or consult, is the intuition of the reader. Someone who knows all the ins and outs of the Tarot but has not taken the time to develop their intuition might be able to give advice which sometimes coincides with the client's question based on which cards are drawn from the deck, but a good reader will consistently give relevant, useful and worthwhile advice.

In terms of personal and spiritual development, divination can help clarify if you are on the right path and offer insights into the choices and decisions you make in life. Tarot cards can be a great meditative tool and some witches go through the whole pack with a different card being meditated upon each day to more fully understand the card and the message it gives. Runes, tarot, angel cards and the ogham can all be used in this manner. Try drawing a single symbol or card for the day ahead and use the message in a similar way to astrology columns in the papers. If you are drawn to card reading there are literally hundreds of interesting tarot decks to choose from while both runes and the ogham are now available as card decks or wooden and stone sets for casting or perhaps you would be more comfortable and familiar with the set of casting stones you have made yourself.

Whatever you end up doing and whoever you do it for, divination can be a great way of tapping into your deep subconscious for guidance, learning, intuition and advice.

CHAPTER 11

Initiation

Initiation is described by the Collins English dictionary as: the act of initiating or the condition of being initiated; the often secret ceremony initiating new members into an organisation. But is that really all there is to it? A ceremony to join a group or club? In which case why keep it secret?

Initiation has been used for centuries as a way of belonging to a tribe, group, club or clan and it is also used as a rite of passage which marks the transition from childhood to adulthood or from novice to master. The mysteries of adulthood can never truly be understood or known by a child nor can the knowledge and experience of a master be fully understood or experienced by the novice. It takes years to develop real experience and practical knowledge of the advanced stages of any craft and initiation can be seen as a way of marking and acknowledging the time spent dedicating oneself to that development and the level of mastery gained as a result. In some traditions and guilds there is a real sense of pride and achievement in reaching that and initiation can convey that degree of mastery to others as well as to oneself.

Initiation as a witch marks your journey through the path of witchcraft – a way of accepting, acknowledging and recognising your status as a witch. Another reason for initiation is to mark your joining of a particular coven or working group, though an initial dedication ceremony often comes first to confer membership of the group, followed by the coven's initiation ceremonies once any training, development and progression have taken place. It's important to point out that there are differences between independent or eclectic covens and the initiatory covens of the Gardnerian/Alexandrian lines but in general terms, covens normally have three degrees, or levels, each level being marked with an initiation and sometimes with a title. There may be different names for each level but they all boil down to similar meanings. The first degree is the level of novice and is referred to as novitiate, apostle, postulant or simply first degree witch. This is marked with an initiation which is the entry level and marks you out as being a witch and as belonging to the coven. Following this there is training and development to make sure the new member of the coven is familiar with the way the coven carries out their rituals and to make a start on learning about the god and goddess, taking elemental journeys and starting to learn the basics of healing, herbal magic, blending incense or whatever other specialisms the beginner is interested in.

Second degree initiation acknowledges the achievements, learning and development already gained and gives a more advanced status, sometimes called Priest or Priestess, more usually referred to as second degree witch. This initiation recognises the development and progress gained so far and leads into more training though at a more advanced level. Within a coven, initiates at this level would be learning how to lead a ritual from start to finish, take an active part in drama for the Sabbat rites, call down the goddess and god and become more competent in any special interests like tarot, healing or mediumship and will help to train up any first level initiates.

The third degree initiation normally gives the status of high priest and high priestess and at this point, you should know how run a coven, create rituals for the Sabbats, while continuing your development in chosen interests and be able to effectively teach novice and second level initiates. In most traditions, the third degree initiation (and sometimes the second level) entitles a high priestess to leave the group and form her own coven. A new coven hived off in this manner will have strong ties to the first group and a few new first degree or second degree witches might go with the new high priestess. This leaves both groups a little smaller than the original and gives the opportunity for new blood to come along – and in the majority of pagan communities there will be plenty of people who are interested in joining a coven so this dividing of the coven makes way for them to be welcomed into either group.

There are covens which don't work this way and stay as a closed group for years or decades, with everyone developing their individual talents and adding to the experience and cohesion of the group. Initiation by the three degrees is just one way of making progress along your witching path. There are dozens of covens who don't follow a traditional, Gardnerian, style of craft, whereby initiation might only be an acknowledgement of learning or a dedication ceremony for joining the group and there might only be one initiation or perhaps four levels or more. We are nothing if not unique!

There isn't always going to be an experienced high priestess leading the group if it has been formed by like-minded individuals who are starting out together with little or no experience between them. People meeting at open rituals might form a more solid group without having a formal initiation and some covens are very loosely organised with different members meeting whenever they can and others dropping in or out as they move in different social circles. There is nothing wrong with this approach, providing that each member of the group is getting what they need from it.

Solitary witches and those novice witches without a mentor don't always have access to the guidance and support of an experienced coven for development but there are hundreds of open groups around the country and a huge range of books and teachers offering workshops, classes and instructions.

There are initiation ceremonies available on the internet or in books for solitary witches to follow but there seems to be little about solitaries also being able to mark their own levels of learning after that. I believe there is a case for making a dedication ceremony to confirm that you are a witch and then going on to do another initiation after you have built up your experience and gained knowledge, understanding and practice of the craft. A second initiation, and a third if you feel it's necessary, will confirm to the Gods, the Elementals and to your deep inner soul that you are not a beginner any more. Your new status as an experienced witch is recognised and you can be proud of that, regardless that it may be something only you know has taken place.

There is a lot to be said for initiation both to acknowledge your entry into witchcraft – a way of stating and confirming that you are a witch – but also to mark your progress as you develop your skills, knowledge, practice and experience. The vast majority of witches, either solitary or those in covens, do carry on developing their practice, learning more and more about their favourite mythologies and deities, achieving better results with rituals and spell casting, closer connections to nature and the cycles of life. The longer you have practiced, the more often you cast a circle or journey to meet the elements, the more advanced and experienced you become as a witch and this dedication deserves recognition.

Self-initiation is quite common, although it used to be frowned upon and pooh-poohed by some as not being a 'proper' initiation. Things have moved on since the early days of the witchcraft revival and now self-initiation is seen by the majority as widely acceptable. Any initiation ceremony, however, must be meaningful and relevant to the initiate so please take what you want from the example below, leave out the rest and add in anything else that speaks to your soul.

Solitary Initiation Ceremony

This ceremony is an example of self-initiation that you can follow as it's set down or adapt to suit your requirements as you please. Where you are doing this as a first step, something akin to the ritual provided will suffice; for those with more experience who are marking their development, progress and learning, alter the wording, add in a phrase or two about what you have learned and be proud to mark this as the second or third initiation that you have earned.

As always, preparation in advance will help you along so read ahead and make sure you're comfortable with these words or make up your own vows for your initiation. There is no need to memorise this either, as you can put this on your altar to read out. Decide if you want to have a magical craft name to use during your circles and if there are any witchy gifts you want to have for your initiation – a crystal wand or a magpie feather, it's up to you. Choose your clothes and jewellery carefully or wear none, cleanse your space with incense or a smudging bundle and then cleanse yourself, starting with a ritual bath or shower and cleanse your energy field. Set up a sacred space to work in and place everything you will need inside it.

And now you are ready to set up the sacred space, cast the circle, perform your invocations to the elementals of air, fire, water, earth and spirit. Offer your invocations and welcome the god and goddess to your sacred rite.

Stand at your altar and hold your arms up high and spread wide, saying:

Great Mother goddess, I call on you to witness this rite of my initiation into the craft of the wise. Bless me as I start my journey, guide my thoughts and deeds with wisdom and grace. Maiden, Mother and Crone, bear witness as I take my vows of witchcraft.

Now make the horned god symbol with your fists (thumb and two middle fingers tucked in, little and forefinger straight).

Horned god of the ancient ways, I call on you to witness this ritual of initiation as I take my vows on the path of witchcraft. Guide my feet in the ways of nature's wisdom and bless my journey. Horned god, hunter and hunted, bear witness to my initiation as a witch.

Now turn to each direction in turn, going round the circle deosil to take the elemental symbol from the altar to offer up at each quarter, holding it high:

Elements of Air in the east (and other elements in turn), I call on you to witness my initiation as a witch. Bless me with your insights, guidance and grace. So mote it be.

Now sit comfortably in silence and meditate for a time on what it means to you to be a witch, how you will live your life and fill your expectations of what witchcraft and initiation will bring to you. Open your heart and soul to the elementals, to the god and goddess.

When you are ready, rise and stand at your altar:

I (name) hereby dedicate myself to the path of witchcraft and paganism. I promise to live with purpose and integrity, to honour my brother and sister witches, to learn the secrets of magic and power and healing. I pledge myself to this path in the name of the triple goddess of the moon and the horned god, let all spirits and elements and deities here present bear witness to my initiation.

I give myself the name of (witch name) to honour my new life as a witch and priest/ess of the old religion.

I accept this gift (take your gift or token from the altar) as a token of my initiation and do hereby consecrate this with the elements of air, fire, water, earth and spirit.

Now place this back on the altar and pick up your chalice.

In the name of the mother goddess and the horned god, I am initiated as a witch and priest/ess. As I do will, so mote it be.

Drink from the chalice and have a piece of bread or cake from the altar and, if outdoors, sprinkle the rest on the ground as an offering.

I (new name) give my thanks to the goddess and god for accepting me as a witch and priest/ess. With the blessings of air, fire, water and earth, with the guidance of spirit and the love of the Old Ones, as I do will, so mote it be!

Coven Dedication Ceremony

Dedication into the coven and to the craft in general is about opening oneself to change and committing oneself to further growth and development. In readiness for this, it is common practice that at the Esbat/Sabbat prior to dedication, the dedicant commits to do some work in preparation. This can be a commitment to the earth and or the craft, a commitment to help others, or to develop particular skills. A token gift to each coven member can be offered, matching pendants, a goddess symbol or a meaningful rune for example. My own experience is that some small token of the coven helps to bring people together and gives a sense of ownership and belonging to the group. This ritual is offered for use by independent or eclectic covens as other traditions, such as Gardnerian Wicca, have specific ritual texts of their own.

Have unlit candles and coven tokens on altar for each dedicant and everyone present should be cleansed/smudged prior to the ritual. The new dedicants should stand in front of altar with Priest and Priestess either side of it. The circle is cast as usual with the elements, god and goddess invoked.

Priestess: *Welcome (name) You have had time to get to know us and to prepare yourself for dedication – do you still want to become a Covener of this group?*

Dedicant: *Yes, I do.*

Priest: *What is the name you have chosen for yourself as a witch?*

Dedicant: I *take the name ….*

Priestess: *Over the last month, what have you done in preparation for your dedication?*

Dedicant: I *have prepared myself spiritually by doing ....*
I have prepared myself mentally by doing......
I have prepared myself physically by doing........

Priest: *Do you have a personal pledge you would like to make?*

Dedicant: *Yes/No*
(can be a poem, a few short words or statement of commitment or an expression of intention – make up your own)

I pledge to the Old Ones, the Lord and Lady,
that I will keep the secrets
of the coven and put my trust in my fellow coveners.
I will work for the good of all and honour my
brother and sister witches as my kin.

Priestess: *Do you, fellow coveners, accept ..... as a suitable member of the group?*

All: *Yes, we accept her.*
(Any objections should have been raised prior to this!)

Priestess: *And do you promise to welcome her always as sister witch and to honour her, support and love and cherish her?*

All: *We welcome you as sister witch and we will honour, support, love and cherish you.*

Priestess: *As priestess of the coven, I greet you as my sister witch.* (Kiss) *I bless you in the name of the Great Goddess*
(She anoints Dedicant with oil over the brow chakra).

Dedicant: *I accept the blessing of the Goddess*

Priest: *I bless you in the name of the Horned God* (anoints)

Dedicant: *I accept the blessing of the Horned God*

Priestess: *Do you promise to always enter our circle with perfect love and perfect trust?*

Dedicant: *I promise to enter only with perfect love and perfect trust.*

Priest: *Are you willing to commit yourself to the group?*

Dedicant: *Yes, I am willing to commit to the group.*

Priestess: *Are you dedicated to continuing your spiritual growth as part of the coven?*

Dedicant: *I am dedicated to my spiritual growth.*

Priestess: *What do you bring in offering to the Goddess and God?*

Dedicant: *I give the goddess and god this offering as a token of my dedication and commitment to the coven.*

(This can be a ring, plant, lock of hair, poem. Place the offering on the altar or read aloud if written. The offering can be buried, burned, given away or kept on the coven's altar according to dedicant's preference.)

Priest: *Are you prepared to accept, support and cherish your fellow coveners, as they will do for you?*

Dedicant: *I will accept, support and cherish them.*

The new coven member should now walk deosil to each member in turn, receiving a kiss, each acknowledging and welcoming one another as member of coven. Dedicant should then return to stand at the altar.

All: *We accept you as a member of the coven.*

Coveners now form an archway with raised hands for the new member to pass through.

Priestess: *Now walk through the archway, leaving your old ways behind and be reborn as you light the candle on the altar, a symbol of rebirth.*

The new member passes through the arch and back to the altar to light a candle.

Priestess: *I offer you this token as a sign of belonging, in perfect love and trust.*

Dedicant: *I accept this token in perfect love and perfect trust.*

Priestess: *I hereby declare you as my sister witch and fellow member of the coven. So mote it be.*

All: *So mote it be, welcome* (new name) *sister witch!*

The ritual is ended as the new covener puts on the token. The priestess should make it her responsibility to facilitate the ritual in any way the dedicant would like (within reason!) and all other coveners should support this and help the dedicant feel comfortable and at ease.

The dedicant could be covered with a dark cloth to represent a cave or death and then emerge to be covered in a light coloured cloth symbolising a new spiritual life. Coveners could surround the dedicant and offer words of friendship as s/he circles among them or the dedicant can write down a few words for everyone to recite; specific goddess and god names can be invoked or the new member might want to burn something they need to get rid of in order to progress. The wording and ritual can be adapted fairly freely but do make sure that all coveners are happy to be joined by this newcomer and that everybody takes an active part in welcoming them to the coven – the idea of a matching coven token is quite well-used and can truly give a sense of belonging. Further dedication or initiation ceremonies can be developed by the coven to recognise the first, second and third degree witches as they progress and learn.

APPENDIX

Ritual Structure

The majority of rites and rituals have the same foundation of working within a sacred space into which the elements and deity are invoked followed by spell casting, poetry or dancing for the sabbat, healing or divination and then raising energy in a cone of power. Rituals end with something to eat and drink and then giving offerings and thanks the elements and deity and closing the circle.

Opening rituals vary from coven to coven and from witch to witch. Change what you don't like, use what you do like and feel free to experiment and explore – see how and why and when and with what tools your rituals seem to be the most powerful. Witchcraft rituals should never be a formula that you reel off parrot-fashion but something that you live and breathe, it is alive and evolving. You will notice that not every element or deity is invoked here with exactly the same words because these invocations and callings into the circle should be intuitive, emotive and fresh. Try it with the words written here, the words that come to your hearts or see if using a longer invocation for the goddess and god as given earlier in the book works well for you or make up your own poems for the elements. Alternatively, you could just wing it and make a note of what happens as you go along so you can use it again if it worked. Having said this, the benefits of memorising text means that the words will flow easily and you won't be desperately trying to think of something clever or impressive to say half-way through your ritual.

Casting the Circle

Place everything you need on your altar; wand, athame, chalice, crystals, candles and lighter, incense, smudge sticks, salt and anything you want to use for spell casting, any offerings or tributes. When calling to the elements, you can leave a token of that element in the appropriate area if desired and then return this to the altar when you give thanks at the end of the ritual later. Start at either the north (earth) or east (air) and walk the perimeter of your area, pointing your wand or athame and imagine a light coming from you to form a barrier, a force-field all around you. Let this light form a shield that goes above you and below you. Imagine the circle forming around you as a silver or golden colour, powder blue or soft pink. Visualisation of the circle is paramount, see it all around your boundary, not as a line but as a bubble or globe going right around, above and below the whole area. Every member of a group should also be visualising this very clearly, backing up the circle caster with their additional energy.

> *I cast this circle as a sacred space, a boundary between the worlds and a container for the energy raised within it. All harmful energy is expelled, letting peace and honesty remain. Let this circle be cast as a place of love and joy and truth. In the name of the Goddess and God, the circle is cast.*

Now invoke the elements. Go to the east quarter of the circle and hold your incense or feather for the element of air, hold it high. As one person invokes and calls in the element, anyone else present should be mentally doing the same.

> *May the spirit of air in the east, the breeze of fresh air, the wind that powers my dreams, element of inspiration and communication, be welcome in this circle, I ask for your presence in my rite. Hale and welcome air.*

Move clockwise to the south quarter and light the incense or an orange candle for the fire spirits.

May the spirit of fire in the south, element of desire, passion, transformation, anger and love, the fire of warmth and creativity, be welcome in this circle. Bear witness and lend your energy to this rite. Hale and welcome fire.

Go clockwise again and pick up the chalice or bowl of water. Stand in the west quarter of your circle.

May the spirit of water in the west, cleansing rain and the tears of release, be present in this circle and stand watch over my rite. Hale and welcome water.

Return to the altar and pick up the stone, pentacle or whatever else you have to represent earth. Go to the north quarter, hold it high.

May the spirit of earth in the north, the element of grounding and stability, guardian trees and healing caves, be present in my circle and witness this ritual. Hale and welcome earth.

Now go back to your altar and face the centre, lifting your head high and raising your hands to the sky.

May the element of spirit, that which binds us all and keeps us whole, the guiding spirit of all that connects us to everyone and everything, be present in this circle. Lend your energy to this rite. Hale and welcome spirit.

Next light the altar candles, again walking clockwise to the altar.

I light this candle for the goddess Cerridwen and ask for her presence in my ritual. She who is love, beauty and mother of us all, great goddess, lend your power to our rite, hale and welcome Cerridwen.

I light this candle for the horned god Cernunnos. I ask for your presence in my ritual. You who are protective and strong, father of us all, lend your power to our rite, hale and welcome Cernunnos.

The circle is now cast and any ritual and magical work is carried out – this could be an enactment of the dance of the gods for one of the sabbats, a healing spell, divination or candle magic.

Next, raise a cone of power through chanting, drumming, dancing, clapping, deep breathing or summoning power and energy from the core of the earth upwards. Release the cone of power only when it reaches a great peak and immediately direct it towards your goal.

This should be followed by blessing of the traditional cakes and ale, or chocolate biscuits and fruit juice, have whatever you like but never eat or drink the last of anything – save some to take outside and offer to the Old Ones after you've closed the circle.

Closing the Circle

The circle is put away for future use in much the same way as it was created, reversing the order in which things are done, including the direction in which you walk round the circle. Deosil, (clockwise) to cast and Widdershins (anti-clockwise) to close.

I give my thanks to the the horned god Cernunnos, father of all life, for your presence in my circle. I bid you Hale and Farewell. I give my thanks to the goddess Cerridwen, mother of all life, for your presence in my circle. I bid you Hale and Farewell.

Move to the centre of your circle and say:

Element of Spirit, I give my thanks for your presence in my circle. I bid you Hale and Farewell.

Stand at the altar in the North, this time thanking the guardians of earth:

Element of Earth in the North, the ground upon which I stand, I thank you for standing watch over my circle. I bid you Hale and Farewell.

Walk to the west and hold your hands high:

> *Element of Water in the West, cleansing rain and refreshing dew, the blood running through my veins, I give my thanks for your presence in this circle. I bid you Hale and Farewell.*

Now continue to the South and give thanks to fire:

> *Element of Fire in the South, the passion in my heart, I offer you my thanks and bid you Hale and Farewell.*

Walk to the east, breathe deeply and thank the air elementals, saying:

> *Element of Air in the East, the breath of life, I give my thanks for your presence in this circle. I bid you Hale and Farewell.*

Walk anti-clockwise around your Circle, pointing your finger at the perimeter. As you walk around see all the light of the circle dissipating into the earth, gently dissolving away. Say something like this:

> *The circle returns to the source of all life, to the ether from where it came, releasing the energy raised within. May love and joy and truth remain. The circle is open. So mote it be.*

If you are working with a group, stand together holding hands and repeat this chant with happiness, swinging your arms up high as you swear to each other that you will meet again.

> *May the circle be open, yet unbroken, may the love of the goddess be ever in our hearts. Merry meet and merry part and merry meet again.'*

Consecration

To consecrate something is to make it sacred, to give it a purpose that lies outside the ordinary and mundane and set it aside for a specific function. This could be your athame, a wooden spoon for kitchen magic, your pagan jewellery, a set of tarot cards or the candles and crystals you will use for your spells and rituals. Consecration should always take place within a circle. Put everything you are using or consecrating on the altar which is set up with candles for fire, incense or feather for air, a chalice or bowl of water, and a piece of wood, stone or your pentacle for earth. Normally, the athame is the first item in the magical tool kit to be consecrated, though everything is consecrated in the same way after that.

Hold the athame in both hands and slightly above the incense so that it is caught in the drift of air or if you have a feather on your altar then use this to create a draught of air around the athame and say:

In the name of the element of air, I bless and consecrate this athame.

Now repeat this with each of the other elements in turn, making sure to hold it against the earth, run it quickly through the heat of the candle's flame and sprinkle lightly with water. Then hold it up high and say:

In the name of the element of spirit which connects and binds us all together, I bless and consecrate this athame. I consecrate this athame as a magical tool, set aside for this purpose and no other, in the name of the Lord and Lady, so mote it be.

Now take your newly consecrated item and hold it close to you, willing a little of your essence into it and if at all possible it should be used straight away.

Magical Correspondences

Air is the element of the east, associated with dawn, springtime, birth and childhood, the breath of life, birds, feathers, incense, clouds, dreams, divination, planning, beginnings, communication, thought, inspiration, the colours blue, yellow and white, the wand on the altar, the festivals of Imbolc and Ostara. Air magic can use balloons, paper planes, feathers, incense, a fan, breathing exercises, chanting and singing, aromas and oil burners, cloud magic.

Fire is the element of the south, associated with high noon, summer time, youthfulness, the blood in our veins, the censor and candles, fire, flames, desires, love, passion, anger, motivation, action, intentions, the colours red, orange and gold, the athame on the altar and the festivals of Beltane and Litha. Fire magic is done with candles, incense, cooking, burning offerings and written spells and solar magic.

Water is the element of the west, associated with dusk, autumn, maturity, balance, the ebb and flow of life energy, emotions, healing, cleansing, tears of sorrow and joy, movement, solace, comfort, divination, the colours blue, grey and green, the chalice on the altar and the festivals of Lammas and Mabon. Water magic uses scrying, cleansing rains, consecrating and charging water, healing, rivers, streams, the sea, sea-shells and moon magic.

Earth is the element of the north, associated with midnight, midwinter, old age and death, decay, renewal, rebirth, strength, growth, protection, stability, the colours brown, green and black, the pentagram on the altar and the festivals of Samhain and Yule. Earth magic includes the use of stones, pebbles, trees, caves, burying things, flowers and plants, planting seeds, ribbons, poppets, clouties and crystal magic.

Love magic – Friday, Venus, the chalice on the altar, rose quartz, full moon and midday, the goddesses Freya, Aphrodite, the tarot card of the lovers, the heart chakra, the Ogham Quert (apple), the rune ken, the colours red and pink, rose petals and rose essential oil, cinnamon incense, love heart symbols.

Healing – Monday, the Moon, white and silver or pale pink and green, the new moon and dawn, the crystals clear quartz and prehnite, the solar plexus chakra, the element of earth, the goddess Brighid, the tarot card Strength, the Ogham Saille (willow), the rune Gebo/Gifu.

Good Luck and Happiness – Sunday, the Sun, gold, silver and orange, the full moon, the Ogham Ur (heather), jasmine incense, the element of fire, the root chakra, amber, citrine and tiger's eye crystals, the rune Wunjo/Wynn, the goddess Diana.

Wealth and Prosperity – Tuesday, Mars, yellow, gold and silver, the Maneki Neko (the Japanese waving cat statue) silver coins or jewels, frankincense, the sacral chakra, mustard seeds, a money plant, the Bagua coin, Herkimer diamond and jasper crystals, the god Ganesha, the runes Birkana and Fehu and the Ogham Beith (birch).

Divination and Psychic Ability – the Moon, the element of water, nag champa and patchouli incense, lilac and purple, the crystals amethyst, bloodstone and smoky quartz, the herbs rosemary, mugwort and yarrow, mirrors and silver, the Ogham Coll (hazel) and rune Eihwaz, the third eye and crown chakras, the goddess Ceridwen or Hecate.

Career and Success/Victory - Wednesday, Mercury, the colours green and brown, the rune Tyr and Ogham Nuinn (ash), an arrow, the element of earth, the pentacle on the altar, a lion or horse, cedar incense, ginger root and saffron, the god Hermes or Mercury.

INDEX